FROM TOM PETERS . . .

He Has a Point. (A Damn Good One.)

While passing the time in the Atlanta airport, I picked up a book on making presentations, *The Exceptional Presenter*, by Timothy Koegel. . . . My reasons for the purchase were selfish: I figure that the odds are high that I'll find at least one, small, operational piece of advice and indeed I did find a couple of new ideas and a ton of always useful reminders.

But there was one enormous point Koegel makes that is ever-so-obvious except that I've never seen it made with such impact and clarity. Are you breathless with anticipation? Well, you should be. Here goes: "Those who practice improve. Those who don't, don't."

Reprinted with permission of Tom Peters Company

Full original blog article available at www.tompeters.com

PRAISE FOR *THE EXCEPTIONAL PRESENTER*

"Our entire staff read *The Exceptional Presenter* as part of our corporate-wide training program. We are now much more comfortable and professional in presentations to groups of 2 or 200."

—**Julie Curtin**, Partner, Development Counsellors International

"In our experience, job candidates who embrace the techniques in Tim's book are more successful when seeking new positions."

—**Tom Gilman**, President and CEO, Baldwin Gilman, Recruiting and Search Professionals

"The single best business investment I have ever made, bar none!"

—**Richard Branning**, Managing Director, Jones Lang LaSalle

"What a terrific resource!"

—**Bill Frist**, M.D., 23rd U.S. Senate Majority Leader

THE EXCEPTIONAL
PRESENTER

THE EXCEPTIONAL PRESENTER

A PROVEN FORMULA TO **OPEN UP!** AND OWN THE ROOM

TIMOTHY J. KOEGEL

GREENLEAF
BOOK GROUP PRESS

Published by Greenleaf Book Group Press
4425 S. Mo Pac Expy., Suite 600, Austin, TX 78735
www.theexceptionalpresenter.com

Distributed by Greenleaf Book Group LP

For ordering information or special discounts for bulk purchases, please contact
Greenleaf Book Group LP at S. Mo Pac Expy., Suite 600, Austin, TX 78735,
(512) 891-6100

Design and composition by Greenleaf Book Group LP
Cover design by Greenleaf Book Group LP

Publisher's Cataloging-In-Publication Data
(Prepared by The Donohue Group, Inc.)

Koegel, Timothy J.
  The exceptional presenter : a proven formula to open up! and own the room /
Timothy J. Koegel.

   p. : ill. ; cm.

  ISBN-13: 978-1-929774-44-9
  ISBN-10: 1-929774-44-3

1. Business presentations. 2. Public speaking. I. Title.

HF5718.22 .K64 2007
658.4/52 2007920959

Printed in the United States of America on acid-free paper

07 08 09 10 11 12 13   10 9 8 7 6 5 4 3

To Amy, Kaitlyn and Marty with whom I am grateful and honored to share life's journey.

To Mom and Dad, for your love, support and encouragement.

Illustration by and in memory of Paul Koegel.

CONTENTS

ACKNOWLEDGMENTS

Thank you:

To Cheryl Drake: For your expertise in editing *The Exceptional Presenter*. Check out Cheryl's services at www.editingplusmore.com.

To Amy Snyder: For your work on my dust jacket picture. You do great work! Sorry about the cracked lenses. See the range of Amy's photographic ability at www.paintedzebraphotography.com.

To Rick Buehner, a true friend and marketing guru: Your advice kept me on course. Visit www.fourteen-14.com to review Rick's marketing and product development consulting services.

To Tom Holtkamp: Your illustrations clearly demonstrate the impact of non-verbal communication. For more of Tom's work visit www.tomholtkamp.com.

FROM THE AUTHOR

The Exceptional Presenter provides the essential skills, techniques and strategies necessary for you to present yourself and your ideas at an exceptional level, to any audience, in any venue.

You can read it on a flight from D.C. to Dallas, on the treadmill or in small doses at night before bed. It reads more like a presentation than a textbook, including stories, examples, bullet points, exercises, performance tracking, note pages and practice charts.

Consistently exceeding an audience's expectations is a hallmark of all exceptional presenters. Therefore, use this book often, especially before major presentations, as a Coach/Mentor to inspire you to rise to the occasion.

The format of the book is concise, focusing only on the core information and allowing you to use it as a quick reference. Highlight it. Mark it up. Document your observations and communication experiences.

Make this book your personal presentation diary and carry it with you on your journey to becoming exceptional!

—Tim Koegel

THE EXCEPTIONAL
PRESENTER

CHAPTER ONE
THE EXCEPTIONAL PRESENTER

BECOMING AN EXCEPTIONAL PRESENTER seems to be a Herculean task. There's a lot to remember. Say this. Move that. Speak up. Look at the audience. Don't fidget. You leave the meeting wondering, "Did I connect? Was I clear? Was that guy sleeping, or was he praying for my presentation to end?"

There are a lot of "experts" out there who will give you all the answers. Type into a leading Internet search engine the words "public speaking," and you'll get 84,300,000 listings. It can be overwhelming. After a while it all seems to sound the same.

The formula you are about to learn will take the mystery and the misery out of presenting. We will break down the art of presenting into a series of skills. Then you will learn a systematic approach to mastering each skill.

Some may argue that when it comes to presentation skills, "You either have it or you don't." Based on my two decades as a presentation coach, I respectfully and wholeheartedly disagree with that statement. I've worked with far too many people who have dramatically improved their presentation effectiveness.

Can anyone become an exceptional presenter? My answer is "Yes" for the vast majority of people who have a desire to improve, a formula to guide their progress and a willingness to develop the skills that comprise the "it" in "You either have *it* or you don't."

The objectives of this book are straightforward and achievable:

1. Provide a proven formula that will enable you to communicate at an exceptional level, in any venue, to any audience.

2. Share practice methods that help you develop skills that will not fail under pressure.

3. Serve as your personal diary to document your improvement.

Look up the word "exceptional" in a thesaurus. Synonyms include: superior, outstanding, excellent, extraordinary and wonderful. Antonyms include: average, ordinary, run-of-the-mill, commonplace and mundane.

Notice that the synonyms did not include: perfect, flawless, unblemished or error-free.

Have you attended any presentations lately? How many of those presentations would you describe as: "superior," "outstanding," "excellent," "extraordinary" or "wonderful"? How many would you describe as: "average," "ordinary," "run-of-the-mill," "commonplace" or "mundane"? What descriptive words do people use to describe your presentations?

No two people are exactly the same when it comes to presentation style, comfort level or expertise. Every presenter and every presentation is unique. *The Exceptional Presenter* is not designed to wrestle you into a pre-selected style. It is intended to complement and enhance your existing style and help you attain the cascade of benefits that come from developing exceptional presentation skills.

The benefits will affect every aspect of your life. Your presentation skill level will affect your income and career track. It will affect your personal relationships and your ability to lead and persuade others. It will affect what job you land and what reputation you build.

Becoming an exceptional presenter is NOT a Herculean task. In fact, it's not a task at all. It is a journey that I believe you will find to be enjoyable, energizing and rewarding.

WHAT MAKES A PRESENTER EXCEPTIONAL?

Write down the names of two exceptional presenters, living or deceased. Select a media personality, an athlete, a politician, a professor or perhaps a business or religious leader.

What characteristics make them exceptional? List four characteristics or traits for each person.

Exceptional presenter #1: _____

Characteristics: _____

_____

_____

_____

Exceptional presenter #2: _____

Characteristics: _____

_____

_____

_____

In the last twenty years I've asked more than 10,000 workshop participants to fill out the form you just filled out. The results open the door to understanding what makes people stand out as presenters. The results have enabled me to develop a formula that turns average presenters into exceptional presenters.

Our next step is to discover what it means to OPEN UP! and Own the Room.

OPEN UP!

OPEN UP! is an acronym representing the six characteristics shared by exceptional presenters. The secret is not just knowing the characteristics, but understanding how to incorporate them into your presentation style.

The Exceptional Presenter is:

Organized

Exceptional presenters take charge! They look poised and polished. They sound prepared. You get the sense that they are not there to waste time. Their goal is not to overwhelm, but to inform, persuade, influence, entertain or enlighten. Their message is well structured and clearly defined.

Passionate

Exceptional presenters exude enthusiasm and conviction. If the presenter doesn't look and sound passionate about his or her topic, why would anyone else be passionate about it? Exceptional presenters speak from the heart and leave no doubt as to where they stand. Their energy is persuasive and contagious.

Engaging

Exceptional presenters do everything in their power to engage each audience member. They build rapport quickly and involve the audience early and often. If you want their respect, you must first connect.

Natural

An exceptional presenter's style is natural. Their delivery has a conversational feel. Natural presenters make it look easy. They appear comfortable with any audience. A presenter who appears natural appears confident.

As an Exceptional Presenter, you must:

Understand Your Audience

Exceptional presenters learn as much as they can about their audience before presenting to them. The more they know about the audience, the easier it will be to connect and engage.

Practice

Those who practice improve. Those who don't, don't. Exceptional skills must become second nature.

Practice is the most important part of the improvement process. If your delivery skills are second nature, they will not fail under pressure.

There are hundreds of opportunities every day to practice the skills in this book. The only thing you need is the desire to practice. Most people never practice. If they do, it's on their way to present a proposal, interview for a job, deliver a keynote presentation or sell an idea to their boss. The time to practice is not in "live," win-or-lose situations. The time to practice is during your normal daily routines, when habits can be formed and mistakes are not costly.

Throughout this book I will highlight daily practice opportunities. You will be surprised at how convenient and how easy practicing can be.

OWN THE ROOM

Own the room is a term describing an actor who is so completely into character that he walks on stage with total confidence. He owns the room.

Owning the room is what will happen for you once you have developed an OPEN communication style. You will present with total confidence and maintain the highest level of professionalism, even in the most challenging circumstances. You will hold yourself accountable for the success or failure of your presentations. And you will do whatever it takes to ensure that your audience understands and remembers your message.

Chapters Four through Nine will show you in detail how to OPEN UP! and Own the Room.

Exceptional Presentation Skills Win Elections

Whether you agreed or disagreed with him, President Bill Clinton was and still is an excellent example of where exceptional presentation skills can take your career. Ask his 1992 and 1996 opponents, George H. Bush and Bob Dole, if presentation skills played a role in the outcome of those two Presidential elections. Both Bush and Dole were highly intelligent, both were World War II veterans and both were scandal free. They each brought vast experience to their campaigns. But despite their credentials, neither could match the presentation skills of William Jefferson Clinton.

From the first question of his first presidential debate, Bill Clinton "owned the room." When the first question was directed his way, candidate Clinton walked toward the lady who had asked the question. He squared his shoulders to her. He looked her straight in the eye and asked her to repeat her name. Then he answered her question. He was connecting from the opening bell.

In the days following presidential debates, I will survey participants in my workshops to find out how much they remembered from the debate. Typically they don't remember much. They'll remember a one-liner or a gaffe. They'll remember questions related to a topic near and dear to their hearts (the environment, education, nuclear arms, Social Security). But despite the fact that they remembered little of what was said, they always have an opinion as to who won. "He carried himself like a president." "He was unflappable." "He connected with me." "He seemed more knowledgeable."

The first televised debate took place in 1960 between candidates Richard Nixon and John Kennedy. The polls following the debate were telling. The majority of people who listened to the debate on the radio thought Nixon had won. The majority of those who watched the debate on TV thought Kennedy had won.

Kennedy looked sharp. He looked fresh. His presence was charismatic. Richard Nixon, on the other hand, had not shaved prior to the debate. His five o'clock shadow caused him to appear tired and a bit haggard. In a video taken prior to the debate Nixon could be heard saying, "Guess I should have shaved." That was the understatement of the evening.

Nixon also decided not to use make-up because he overheard Kennedy refusing make-up. He did not know that Kennedy had been made up earlier in the evening.

Flash to the 1992 debate between President George H. Bush, Bill Clinton and Ross Perot. During the town hall debate President

Bush glanced at his watch several times. Years later in an interview with Jim Lehrer, President Bush admitted that glancing at his watch reinforced a mistaken general perception that his heart wasn't 100% into the campaign.

In the first Election 2000 debate it was Al Gore's behavior that damaged his effectiveness. He sighed loudly when he disagreed with then Governor George W. Bush. He interrupted and rolled his eyes repeatedly. His behavior overshadowed anything he had to say about domestic or foreign issues.

The highlight of John Kerry's 2004 run for the White House and the worst performance of the Bush campaign happened the night of the first Presidential debate.

The normally mechanical Kerry appeared relaxed and conversational. His posture at the lectern was commanding. He seemed well prepared. He looked and sounded like someone who could be President.

President Bush leaned on his lectern throughout the debate. Leaning on the lectern had become a campaign stump speech habit for the President, and it carried into the debate. It made him appear tired and a bit uninterested.

Frequent facial expressions suggested that President Bush was agitated or frustrated with his opponent, yet the President did not verbally counter punch. Excessive filler, "ums" and "uhs," combined with the overuse of certain phrases led to the impression that the President was armed with twelve minutes of information for a ninety-minute debate. The President's six to eight point poll lead disappeared.

A much more prepared, passionate and commanding President Bush showed up for debates two and three. He was able to regain his momentum and win the election.

Two Lessons from Election 2004:

1. Every presentation counts! Every handshake, every interview, every appearance, every debate and every one-on-one encounter represents an opportunity to make a favorable impression while driving home a message. Don't allow yourself to miss a single opportunity. It has meant the difference between becoming The President of the United States and becoming a retired ex-politician.

2. Never let your competition back in the game by allowing yourself to present/communicate at a level that is less than exceptional.

>> Delivering an exceptional presentation will not guarantee a win every time. But you should never lose because your presentation was less than exceptional.

CHAPTER TWO
IT'S NOT WHERE YOU START, IT'S WHERE YOU FINISH

THERE HAS NEVER BEEN A MORE IMPORTANT TIME to possess exceptional presentation skills. We've moved from an economy where businesses faced local, regional and national competition to an economy where businesses face stiff competition at every level from around the globe.

Business leaders tell me that instead of competing against two or three firms, they now face four to six firms proposing for the same assignment. The margin of error has vanished. Missteps and missed opportunities are costly.

Every year *The Wall Street Journal* (WSJ) publishes its Corporate Recruiters Survey. The survey ranks business schools based on the input it receives from corporate recruiters, the people who interview and hire MBA students. One part of the survey includes the attributes recruiters list as "very important" for MBA job candidates. The hiring attribute consistently found at the top of the list is communication/interpersonal skills.*

Recruiters rated the business schools and their M.B.A. students on 21 attributes. Here is a list of the 10 highest attributes from the most recent *Wall Street Journal* Corporate Recruiters Survey and the percentages of recruiters who listed these attributes as "very important":

89.0%   Communication/interpersonal skills

86.9%   Ability to work well within a team

86.2%   Personal ethics and integrity

84.3%   Analytical and problem-solving skills

82.9%   Work ethic

74.5%   Fit the corporate culture

74.0%   Success with past hires

72.5%   Leadership potential

67.1%   Strategic thinking

64.9%   Likelihood of recruiting "stars"

People who possess exceptional communication skills maintain a distinct competitive advantage in winning new business and securing the best jobs. In an unforgiving economy their advantage becomes even more pronounced.

A client in San Francisco takes full advantage of his presentation prowess. His strategy is to force his competition into a beauty contest, where he and his competitors present their capabilities and solutions to the prospect. As he puts it, "Most of my competitors don't like to present, they don't know how to prepare, and most are not good presenters. If I can present to the prospect at

---

* Wall Street Journal/Harris interactive ranking of America's Top Business Schools: Corporate Recruiter's M.B.A. picks.

any stage in the selection process, I have a good chance of winning the assignment."

DO NOT DISCOUNT YOUR POTENTIAL AS A PRESENTER.

I've helped thousands of people communicate more powerful messages to their prospects, voters, employers, investors and the media. I've consulted at the White House, in boardrooms, at business schools and CEO boot camps, from Capitol Hill to Silicon Valley. Wherever I go, or whomever I work with, one fact remains consistent: **No matter what your skill level—no matter what your presentation comfort level—you can become exceptional.**

Take Lee, a design and construction specialist in Dallas. Lee initially rated himself a 3 on a scale of 1-10 (10 being the best). He now consistently presents in the 8-9 range, and he looks forward to presentations rather than trying to avoid them.

The turning point for Lee was watching his presentations on video tape. As he worked on his techniques, he could review the tape and witness immediate positive change. The changes were not yet consistent, but for the first time, Lee could see his presentation potential, and he was determined to tap that potential. Lee has indeed tapped his potential, and his more effective presentation style has enabled him to achieve a higher income level, greater respect as an industry expert and a reputation in his office as a "must-have-on-the-team" for major proposals.

Or Carol, an investment advisor in Indianapolis. Nervousness nearly caused Carol to pass out any time she rose to speak. Carol now presents with poise and confidence. Her nerves are no longer a barrier to her communication efforts, and her speaking skills are creating new sources of revenue and relationships. For Carol, knowing that she looked and sounded more confident enabled her to feel more confident.

Even one of the greatest speakers of the 20th Century, Winston Churchill, had to overcome fears and limitations. Still, he said, "There are only a few things in life from which I derive intense pleasure, speaking is not one of them!"

The Exceptional Presenter is not a complex book. It's not rocket science. Rather, it's rocket fuel—some helpful tips designed to lift your skills to new heights. In fact, you will learn that presenting is quite basic. Once we break down the components of presenting, mastering those components becomes as easy as practice and repetition.

DO NOT UNDERESTIMATE THE POWER OF YOUR DELIVERY.

Dr. Albert Mehrabian conducted research at UCLA to find out what factors influence the perception of our spoken message. The results are important to our understanding of presentation effectiveness.

His research revealed that when communicating feelings and attitudes:

7% of an audience's perception of our message is determined by our words

38% by our voice

55% by our non-verbals

What can we take from Mehrabian's controlled study to help us become exceptional presenters? I believe the key point is this: Voice and non-verbal communication greatly impact our ability to influence and persuade. They will either raise or lower our level of expertise, intelligence and trustworthiness in the minds of the audience.

If our non-verbal communication contradicts, rather than supports, our message, we can be confident, yet look nervous and tentative. We can be prepared, yet look woefully unprepared. We can be an expert, yet have the presence of a novice. We can be passionate, yet appear apathetic. We can be genuine, yet sound insincere. On the other hand, through the use of stronger delivery techniques, we can be perceived as being more prepared, more of an expert, and more confident than perhaps we are. Exceptional presenters know how to use both vocal and physical delivery to their advantage.

As former Chrysler Corporation Chairman Lee Iacocca once said, "You can have brilliant ideas, but if you can't get those ideas across, they don't do anybody any good."

DO NOT UNDERESTIMATE HOW OFTEN YOU USE THESE SKILLS.

Adopt a broader definition of "presentation skills" to include any form of oral communication. I frequently hear the following comment, "I only present once or twice a year. I don't use these skills very often." That's not true.

>> Every time you open your mouth to speak in public, you are a public speaker.

Every time you utter a phrase within earshot of another human being, you are making an impression. Even when you listen, your body language is projecting a message back to the other person.

Circle the situations from the list on the following page in which you have found yourself speaking and/or listening:

Proposals	Prospecting calls	Job interviews
Customer service	Negotiating	Training
IPO road shows	TV appearances	Fund raising
Social functions	Client reviews	Banquets
Conversations	Brainstorming	Recruiting
Teleconferences	Board meetings	Mentoring
Parenting	Sharing your vision	Arguing
Debating	Gossiping	Teaching
Sales meetings	Staff meetings	Voice mail
Networking	Phone calls	Instructing others
Counseling	Cold calls	Keynote speeches
Introducing others	Team presentations	Product launches
Account meetings	Q&A sessions	Hosting an event
Reading at services	Luncheons	Questioning clients
Selling products	Updating superiors	Coaching
Talking with spouse	Talking with peers	Convention booths

All of these venues should be included in your new definition of presentations.

I suspect you have multiple circles on the page. Even if you have only one, you can still benefit from the techniques in this book.

A CASCADE OF BENEFITS AWAITS THE EXCEPTIONAL PRESENTER

Get excited about what you can achieve with these skills. The end result of exceptional presentation skills can be seen in the following list of benefits clients have told me they have experienced:

- Build a reputation as THE preeminent authority.

  Dateline: Chicago—A senior manager with a financial services firm was looking to build eminence in the business community for his practice. He pursued opportunities to speak to business groups in Chicago on the topic of corporate fraud. He achieved his goal of building eminence. He also landed several new clients, including one that generated $3.5 million of revenue within fourteen months. The senior manager is now a partner, partly due to his ability to generate new sources of revenue for his firm.

- Leverage your time. Presenting to groups is an efficient way to prospect. Few organizations adopt a strategic approach to this prospecting gold mine.

  Dateline: D.C.—A client accepts an opportunity to deliver a state-of-the-market presentation to a group of 160 CEOs and CFOs. For 45 minutes, the client had the undivided attention of those executives. They have since conducted business with over a dozen of the attendees. Others have requested follow-up meetings. The resulting revenue will stream in for years. How long would it take to schedule separate meetings with 160 CEOs and CFOs? It would be a difficult task.

- Present with confidence to superiors, peers and subordinates.

    Most of us spend a significant amount of time communicating. A higher level of communication confidence will spill over to other aspects of our lives.

- Increase your earning potential. For those in management, the ability to motivate, influence and persuade can open doors. For those in sales, a more competent, confident and conversational presenter will out-sell the typical presenter almost every time.

- Conduct results-oriented meetings. Your attendees will appreciate a well-defined and well-orchestrated meeting that starts and ends on time.

- Win a higher percentage of proposals.

- Become more versatile. The more you can do, the better your chances of staying on the payroll.

- Showcase your story when interviewing. Provide recruiters with a three-dimensional, dynamic and completely engaging picture of your experience and your potential.

- Build credibility within your organization.

- Secure lasting relations with clients and customers.

- Project the image and presence of a leader.

- Increase your ability to influence others.

- Enhance marketability. Organizations can't afford to lose exceptional communicators.

- Make strong first impressions.

- Network more effectively.
- Fast-track your career.
- Become a rainmaker.
- Excel at leading, inspiring and motivating others.

What other benefits might you derive?

_____

_____

_____

A client from Denver recently told me that in addition to boosting his business, these skills have made him a much better Sunday School teacher. He can see the difference in the attentiveness of his young pupils. His improved skills are making a positive difference in the lives of his clients and his students.

HOW ARE YOU POSITIONED AS A PRESENTER?

Experience tells me that 80% of presenters are below average, 10% are average, 5% are good to very good and 5% are exceptional.

The percentage of exceptional presenters can and should be significantly higher. Most presenters never tap their full potential. Most presenters are below average because they:

- Don't seriously commit to improving.
- Don't attend presentation training.
- Don't videotape and critique their presentation style.
- Don't seek objective feedback from an expert.
- Don't have a system to develop productive habits.
- Don't know how to practice.

They're stuck, and their effectiveness or lack thereof will not change.

Exceptional presenters understand that much of their success can be attributed to their superior skills. They're confident in knowing that they maintain a competitive advantage because of their advanced skills. All things being equal (such as experience, education, knowledge, price and service), or as close as you can get to equal, the exceptional presenter is more likely to win the proposal, be offered the job, win the election, retain the client, convince the boss or sell the idea.

If your competitors understand the impact of these skills, and they reach the exceptional level, they will dominate in competitive situations.

I find it fascinating that when conducting presentation skills training sessions, the better the presenter, the more they soak up the material. Perhaps it's because these individuals understand that:

>> How the word is spoken can dramatically impact the power of the spoken word.

These individuals are open to any idea or technique that can sharpen the blade, even a little.

In the front of this book I included portions of a blog article written by management guru Tom Peters. He wrote the article after purchasing and reading *The Exceptional Presenter*. For more than 30 years, Tom Peters has been one of the most sought-after speakers in the world. He speaks with tremendous passion and enthusiasm about business management and performance. He is totally committed to his message and to making sure his audience understands that message.

The first paragraph of the Peters article about *The Exceptional Presenter* speaks volumes as to why he continues to be considered one of the best. It reads:

> "My reasons for the purchase were selfish: I figure the odds are high that I'll find at least one, small, operational piece of advice . . . and indeed I did find a couple of new ideas and a ton of always useful reminders."

Here is one of the top speakers in the world looking for "one, small, operational piece of advice." The top presenters are constantly looking for ways to sharpen the blade. They understand the power and impact of exceptional presentation skills.

While most people simply hope to "get through" the presentation, exceptional presenters prepare and present with their foot on the accelerator and total focus on helping the audience understand their message. The exceptional presenter is always prepared and always looking for ways to refine and improve.

>> If you don't think these skills are critical, keep your fingers crossed that your competition has the same attitude.

CHAPTER THREE
PRESENT TO WIN OR PREPARE TO LOSE

WHAT IS THE COST OF HAVING LESS THAN EXCEPTIONAL or poor presentation skills? No one truly knows. Rest assured, if your skills are lacking, you are losing money, handcuffing your ability to land your dream job, damaging your professional image and derailing your career aspirations.

According to the Association of Fraud Examiners, American businesses lose nearly 5% of annual revenue to internal fraud. Translated into dollars that comes out to a loss of approximately $700 billion annually. It's $700 billion right out the door.

I'd venture to say that the typical American business loses at least 5% of annual revenue due to poor presentation and communication skills.

My accounting clients tell me that when a company learns that it's losing 5% of revenue to fraud, the company immediately puts plans in place to stop the bleeding. It's painful to realize that someone is stealing your hard-earned money. "We'll catch the thieves and throw them in jail," they say. "I don't care what it costs to stop these criminals."

By contrast, losing revenue because of poor presentation skills isn't quite as painful. It's easier to ignore. The money never flowed in. You never had it in the first place. So, we say, "Oh, well, that one got away. We'll get the next one."

Every company should establish an accounting ledger for business they've lost due to poor presentation skills. They have budgets for training, development, travel and entertainment. Why not establish a "blown opportunity" budget each fiscal year? "As soon as we've achieved $15 million in revenue that we should have had, we'll do something to beef up the way we communicate our services."

>> The average presenter's loss is the exceptional presenter's gain.

HOW WAS I TO KNOW? NO ONE EVER TOLD ME!

"Advice is seldom welcome. Those who need it most, like it least."
—Samuel Johnson

How do you know if your presentation skills are lacking? How can you measure your effectiveness if you don't assess your skills? Rarely will someone volunteer honest, pull-no-punches feedback. Most people don't like being the bearer of bad news. On the flip side, most people don't willingly or gracefully accept feedback.

You probably won't hear people say:

"Jim, your speech was pathetic. I assume you didn't have time to practice."

"Sue, we appreciate you coming in and boring us to tears."

"John, I'm curious, have you considered a speech coach?"

"Of all the speakers we've heard, you are, without question, the worst. And we've heard a lot of speakers."

We'd be lucky to hear such comments. If we were lousy, wouldn't we want to know? I'd rather have someone tell me I didn't look prepared, I missed the mark, or that my presentation was boring than have someone pat me on the back and say, "Nice job." A dose of reality can serve as a wake-up call and encourage us to improve the way we present our information.

Senior level executives, politicians and bosses are especially prone to the "Nice job" trap. These individuals are surrounded by a smoke screen of compliments and backslapping delivered by people who don't feel it's their job to shoot straight with the boss. They don't want to fall out of favor, or worse yet, get fired for providing honest feedback. So instead, they say:

"I've never seen you better, sir."

"Wow! That's all I can say, sir."

"You knocked that one out of the park, sir."

Harken back to the Samuel Johnson quote, "Advice is seldom welcome. Those who need it most, like it least." Or as Norman Vincent Peale once put it, "The trouble with most of us is that we would rather be ruined by praise than saved by criticism."

How do you take feedback? Are you open to listening to the honest opinions of others? Or will you "kill the messenger" if the feedback doesn't feed your ego?

Seeking feedback from a presentation coach is an excellent way to assess your skills. Make sure the coach uses videotape to provide feedback. The camera doesn't lie. What you see and hear on tape is what your audience sees and hears. A coach will highlight your strengths and bring attention to those skill sets in need of refinement.

A coach will spot tendencies that an untrained person would miss. Most people can tell a good presentation from a bad presentation. But can they pinpoint specific reasons it was good or bad? Can they readily spot body language that is incongruent with the words being spoken? Can they discern vocal variations that cause an audience to disengage? Can they pick up mannerisms that create negative impressions? Probably not. Professional evaluation is essential.

Eileen thought things were going great. . . . until the laser pointer incident.

THE COST OF AVERAGE ILLUSTRATED

Dateline: Silicon Valley, CA—Bob Marshall, Silicon Valley legend and CEO of Selby Venture Partners, estimates that 80% of start-up companies die with their funding presentations. The company executives are unable to present their technology in a way that investors understand. In addition, 80% of the CEOs are poor presenters. They don't look and sound like business leaders. Would you hand that CEO a $3,000,000 check?

Dateline: Houston, TX—RE Consultants lost three consecutive proposals. Each debriefing elicited the same response: "Your presentation was flat. You didn't look like you wanted our business." RE was stunned. They had devoted significant time and resources to each presentation. RE lost the immediate and ongoing revenue from three substantial assignments. They were unaware of how their presentations were being perceived. They had not practiced on videotape to find out just how uninspiring their presentations appeared.

Dateline: Cincinnati, OH—An investment firm loses a large client as a result of a poor presentation. The client later said, "We couldn't believe you were managing our financial future. You couldn't manage a 45-minute presentation."

Dateline: North Carolina—A real estate developer loses a $100 million project because the person leading the proposal completely disengaged from the prospect by reading the entire presentation word for word.

Dateline: Phoenix—An architect loses a $3.5 million job on the basis of what the prospect called a horrible presentation. The poor showing overshadowed an excellent track

record. The architect said he thought the presentation had
gone quite well.

WHAT IS THE COST OF AVERAGE?

In addition to lost revenue and blown opportunities, the cost of
average is missing out on the cascade of benefits exceptional presentation skills bring. It is more than you can afford.

Fill out the "Rate Yourself as a Presenter" form to objectively
assess your current skill level.

RATE YOURSELF AS A PRESENTER

What are your greatest strengths as a presenter?

_____

_____

_____

An executive once responded: "I really have no strengths, but if I had to list one, I guess it would be humility."

What are your areas of greatest need and refinement?

_____

_____

_____

Are you more comfortable presenting to people you know or people you don't know? _____

What is the difference? _____

Are you a better presenter standing up or sitting down? _____

Do you prefer: a script, bullet points or off the cuff? _____

What impression do you make on an audience? _____

_____

_____

_____

Have you used videotape to critique your effectiveness? _____

If yes, when did you last tape yourself? _____

What did you learn? _____

_____

_____

_____

Rate and evaluate yourself again in 60 days.

CHAPTER FOUR
ORGANIZED: STRUCTURING YOUR STORY

THE INFORMATION THAT FOLLOWS provides a framework that has proven helpful when preparing clients for presentations, proposals, road shows, interviews, media appearances, question and answer (Q&A) sessions, phone conversations and even important voice mail messages.

This framework will help you alleviate some of your pre-preparation anguish and allow you to efficiently and consistently structure a powerful message.

There are two essential facets of organizing a presentation:

1. Develop a **structure** that allows you to frame your objective, cover all relevant material, transition smoothly from topic to topic and finish strong.

2. **Look organized.** If you don't look organized, the perception will be that you didn't care enough to prepare. You create a negative impression right from the start.

A longstanding presentation structure is:

- Tell them what you're going to tell them (opening).
- Tell them (body).
- Tell them what you just told them (close).

It's a good foundation, and in the following pages we will build on this timeless structure.

WHAT DID HE JUST SAY?

Studies suggest that the average adult "undivided attention span" is 15 to 30 seconds.

For those of you who were not paying attention, let me repeat that statistic: The average adult "undivided attention span" is 15 to 30 seconds.

No single topic or speaker can possibly maintain the undivided attention of an audience for very long. The human brain has way too much capacity for information to "stay tuned" to one person. Even if the information is fascinating, the attention of your audience is drifting in and out of the presentation as they relate the information to past, present or future experiences. Some of these experiences have no relationship to the topic. The topic or a word or a tone of voice triggered the brain to think about what to pick up from the grocery store on the way home. Or something the speaker said reminded them of a meeting they have scheduled for tomorrow afternoon. "There's no way I can make that meeting! Let's see. When can I reschedule the call? Hmmm, when is my daughter's recital anyway? Wonder how she's doing in school today? I have to pick up flowers for her recital."

The mind constantly darts in multiple directions. If the presenter does not constantly work to reengage, reengage and reengage, the audience will have little reason to refocus and pay attention.

Most people will forget 95% of what you say within minutes of hearing your message. That's assuming they hear it in the first place.

If you want your message to be heard and remembered:

>> Keep it short. Keep it focused. Keep it relevant.

I worked with a client who was scheduled to speak to his international sales force for 45 minutes. Why 45 minutes? Because that's how much time the conference organizers gave him on the agenda.

I asked him to name the 2 most important pieces of information the sales force should take away from his presentation.

His two takeaways for the sales force:

1. Focus on the things you can control: your daily activities, the number of calls per day, building relationships and being a resource for our clients. Forget about the things you can't control: The economy, pricing, changes in the industry and Wall Street expectations.

2. Raise your daily level of energy and intensity. Have fun. Make every call count.

Did he need 45 minutes to state those two objectives and support his points with an action plan? No. He did it in 7 ½ minutes. He received a standing ovation from a fired-up sales force. He told me that he received more positive feedback about this presentation than any presentation he had ever delivered.

THE FIVE COMPONENTS OF ANY PRESENTATION

Work to make the following five components as concise as possible. Use the five components to frame a 60-second opening for your 20-minute or 2-hour presentation. Use this structure to craft a high-impact 2-minute presentation. If you are scheduled for a media appearance or job interview, use the five components to organize your thoughts, opinions and positions on the various topics that are likely to be discussed during the interview.

Think of a presentation you've recently completed or one that you will soon deliver. Apply the following suggestions to that presentation. Use a proposal, status report, client conversation or keynote speech. This process will be more meaningful if you use material that is "real life." Presentation to: _____

1. Begin with a "Purpose"

"A speech without a purpose is like a journey without a destination."
—Ralph C. Smedley

Picture yourself in front of your audience. Your presentation is about to begin. You are determined that they will remember your key points far beyond the end of the meeting.

Complete the following sentence.

"If you remember just one thing as you leave here today, remember this . . .": _____

_____

_____

By completing that sentence, you have successfully identified the most relevant information in your presentation. As you build the presentation, never lose sight of that one thing. It is your purpose.

Delivering a purpose statement at the beginning of your presentation will keep the audience focused on your key points. It will prepare them for what they are about to hear.

>> If you tell people what they are about to hear, they are more likely to hear it.

The more defined your purpose, the easier it is to frame your message and stick with it. If you clearly define the purpose of your presentation, you will find it easier to keep your information relevant. You will also avoid delving into areas that are better addressed at a different time and place.

2. Objective/Purpose/Mission/Goal

If you have clearly identified the 1, 2, or at most 3 key points you want the audience to remember (Purpose Statement), then you can use your Objective/Purpose/Mission/Goal to identify what you will cover. In other words, what is the agenda? Don't go into detail at this point. Give the audience a 30,000 foot view of your agenda.

> "My objective this afternoon is to examine two new clinical studies that demonstrate. . . ."

> "My purpose today is to introduce our newest product design. . . ."

> "My mission is to help you identify potential issues related to. . . ."

> "My goal in the next 20 minutes is to clarify our position and answer any questions you have regarding. . . ."

Why are we here? What is the agenda?

If you cannot clearly define your objective, then there is probably not a compelling reason to do the presentation. The purpose statement and objective set the agenda.

By defining the objectives/agenda, you signal to your audience that you are organized, prepared and focused. A well-defined objective suggests competence.

3. Position/Situation/Issues

How are things positioned? What is the situation? What are the issues?

Outline the issues, concerns, fears, expectations, successes or obstacles as you understand them.

> "As I understand the situation, you are experiencing rising inventories and declining sales. Your receivables are running at fourteen weeks and you recently lost your biggest

customer. You've determined that you don't have the experience or the resources to turn the situation around."

At this point in your presentation, stop and ask your audience if anything has changed. Are there other issues that are relevant to the discussion?

> "Is there anything else I need to be aware before proceeding?"

> "Jill, since we last spoke, have any of your objectives changed?"

I have seen presenters deliver entire proposals without once stopping to make sure that their understanding of the situation was still accurate. Only after the proposal did they find out that a critical piece of information had changed and their solutions were no longer relevant. The earlier you ask about changes, the easier it is to adjust your presentation accordingly.

4. End Result/Benefits/Consequences

What are the benefits, ramifications, consequences and implications of taking or not taking action?

> "As a result of our falling sales, we've lost 7% market share in the last 12 months."

> "The implication of our increased inventory is that we will be forced to shut down the Jacksonville plant for thirty days."

> "Our focus on efficiency in the last two quarters has resulted in an additional $22 million to our bottom line."

"The benefit of acting on the proposal today will be seen in the form of additional revenue in the next 90 days."

5. Next Step/Action Plan/Time Line

What is the next step? What are the expectations? Where do we go from here?

Use the next step as your call to action. It will help prepare your audience for what you expect of them and what they can expect of you. The next step can be as simple as, "Let's meet again on Wednesday." Or it can set the stage for significant and detailed follow up.

"Our next step is to ramp up marketing efforts in the East."

"Our plan is to launch the new program by April 1st."

"Going forward, I would like you to meet with your team and select a leader to manage the project."

"We need to finalize the contract by Friday."

HOW TO "TELL THEM WHAT YOU'RE GOING TO TELL THEM"

Example: 60-second opening using the five components.

"The key point I would like you to remember today is this: We will be unable to grow as a business unless we correct our inventory inefficiencies.

"My **objective** this afternoon is to persuade you to approve the purchase of the Acme inventory software in order to put an end to our inventory crisis.

"Our current **position** is one of reacting to inventory changes instead of anticipating customer demand. We have recently lost two significant customers because of botched orders. We have an additional problem in that our regional offices are unable to communicate inventory fluctuations to a central location.

"The **end result** of our inventory problem is that we're losing customers and we're losing $3 million per quarter.

"If we upgrade to the Acme software, we will benefit by holding onto the $3 million per quarter, and our more efficient response time will create greater customer loyalty.

"The **next step** is to approve the purchase of the software this afternoon and have it in place within 30 days."

The objective of the meeting is clear. There's no confusion as to how the company is positioned. The cost of inaction and the benefits of taking action are stated up front. Participants understand what the presenter is recommending.

There are other approaches to creating a powerful objective statement. Let's change the order of the components and note the effect.

"The **situation** is as follows. We are using antiquated inventory software. Our response time to customer requests is unacceptable. In addition, our regional offices have no way of communicating inventory status to a central location.

"The **end result** of our inefficiency is that we're losing $3 million per quarter and we're losing customers.

"My **objective** this afternoon is to persuade you to purchase new inventory software immediately in order to correct this situation.

"The three things I'd like you to think about today are 1) Our inventory problem has a strangle hold on our ability to grow as a company. 2) Our existing inventory software isn't getting it done. And 3) We have identified a viable software option that can remedy the situation.

"The **next step** is to approve the purchase of the new Acme inventory software and have it in place within 30 days."

You may have noticed that this arrangement of the five components draws more attention to the objective.

Each opening took less than forty-five seconds to deliver.

FRAME YOUR "REAL LIFE" PRESENTATION

Craft a sixty-second opening consisting of the five components. Use them in any order. Time your completed opening.

Begin each segment with the following words:

If you remember one thing from our session today, remember this:

_____

_____

_____

My objective (purpose, mission, goal) today is

_____

_____

_____

We are currently positioned OR The situation is as follows

_____

_____

_____

The end result (benefit, consequence, ramification)

_____

_____

_____

Our next step

_____

_____

_____

You have just defined your opening and framed your entire presentation.

HOW TO "TELL THEM"

Use the same framework for the body of your presentation where you can go into greater detail. How much time you spend in each segment depends on what you are attempting to accomplish.

Use stories, examples and anecdotes to help fix your message in the minds of your audience. Keep every piece of information relevant. Stay focused on what you want them to remember.

Be sure to work on your transitions from segment to segment. If your information flows smoothly, you will appear more knowledgeable than a presenter who fumbles from one topic to the next.

"Now that we've discussed the benefits of the new system, let's lay out the steps and the timing of implementation."

HOW TO "TELL THEM WHAT YOU JUST TOLD THEM"

Summarize what you have presented to them.

"In summary, our target clients need to fall into one of two categories:

1. _____

2. _____

If we stay true to this plan, we will have more qualified prospects and our win ratio should jump dramatically."

END WITH A PURPOSE STATEMENT

What you say last will be remembered most. We started our presentation framework by establishing a purpose. A purpose statement is an effective way to end your presentation.

The purpose statement provides the one, two or three key points your audience must remember as they leave the room. The shorter and more direct the purpose statement, the greater its impact.

Question and answer sessions can occur during or after your presentation. If you open the floor to questions after your presentation, be sure to end the session by drawing the attention of your audience back to your purpose.

The quality of the questions oftentimes diminishes as Q&A proceeds. Don't end your session on a low note. Don't end your presentation with the final question. Use your purpose statement to hammer home your key points one final time. Make sure your audience remembers the strongest points of your session. You don't want an irrelevant answer to an irrelevant question ringing in their ears as they leave.

Wrap up the Q&A and close your session by delivering your "purpose statement."

> "If there are no further questions, keep in mind that we owe our existence to our customers. Do everything humanly possible to service their every need."

> "If there are no further questions, keep in mind that the destiny of this organization is not a matter of chance, it is a matter of choice. The choices we make in the next 30 days will decide our fate."

At the end of this chapter and in the back of this book are prep sheets that will help you prepare for your next presentation.

ATTENTION-GRABBING OPENINGS

Beginning the presentation with a purpose or objective is both effective and functional. However, exceptional presenters go a step further: they add an attention-grabbing opener. An ineffective opening can handicap your entire presentation. Set the expectations within 60-90 seconds that your message is worth their undivided attention.

Use the first sixty seconds to lay the foundation. This is not the time to go into extensive detail. Use the body of the presentation to delve into as much detail as you need, or as much as time constraints dictate.

If you want to start your presentation with something other than the objective, you have many options from which to choose.

As you become more proficient at structuring your message, you can try more creative and more flexible ways to start your presentation.

- **A quote:**

    "When one door of opportunity closes, another opens; but often we look so long at the closed door that we do not see the one which has been opened for us." —Helen Keller

- **A statistic:**

    "The next time you deliver a speech, keep in mind that 90% of what you're about to say will be forgotten within 60 minutes."

- **A question to the audience:**

    "What is the greatest challenge facing your business today?"

- **A current news item or periodical:**

    "According to today's *Wall Street Journal* . . ."

- **A story that relates directly to your message:**

    Suppose you are speaking on the topic of leadership: "Willie Shoemaker, one of horse racing's greatest jockeys, once said, 'I always tried to keep the lightest possible grip on the horse's reins. The horse never knows I'm there until he needs me.'"

- **A sincere thank you or acknowledgment:**

    "I'd like to thank the Academy for this honor."

- **Have them write something down:**

    "There are six characteristics shared by the world's most exceptional speakers. You probably want to write these down."

- **Humor:**

  President George W. Bush would often begin his campaign stump speeches by saying, "Before I left Texas my wife Laura said to me, 'Honey, don't try to be charming, don't try to be witty, don't try to be eloquent, just be yourself.'"

- **Make a prediction:**

  "By the time you leave here today, I predict that you will have a plan in place to increase your sales by 15% to 20%."

- **A poem or rhyme:**

  "Give me your tired, your poor, Your huddled masses yearning to breathe free, The wretched refuse of your teeming shore. Send these, the homeless, tempest-tost to me. I lift my lamp beside the golden door!" A poem by Emma Lazarus that is graven on a tablet within the pedestal of the Statue of Liberty.

- **An extended pause**

IF YOU DON'T LOOK ORGANIZED, YOU WON'T APPEAR PREPARED

We've all seen a presenter begin his speech by looking down, shuffling notes, hemming and hawing, clearing his throat, testing the microphone and tucking in his shirt. The presenter has had several weeks to prepare; yet he appears completely caught off guard by the fact that it's his turn to speak.

Even if this presenter is a leading authority on the topic, his thirty seconds of floundering sends the opposite signal to his audience. As Tom Peters says, "Perception is reality." The audience sees a presenter who is not prepared. His perceived lack of preparation is interpreted as a lack of respect for his audience. It also creates questions as to his level of confidence in what he is about to present.

We have one chance to make a first impression. Or, as a client in Texas put it, "You have one chance to kiss the pig." Don't fritter away that one chance by appearing unprepared. We begin judging people the instant we make visual contact. Audiences will judge you before you utter your first word.

Do you look prepared?

Stand.

Set your notes.

Establish eye contact.

Pause for 3-4 seconds.

Smile.

State your purpose.

THE 60/20 RULE

Arrive 60 minutes before you are scheduled to present. Use the first 40 minutes to prepare: the room, seating, notes, AV equipment, handouts and props.

The 20 minutes prior to your presentation is prime time for introductions, information gathering and rapport building.

This is not the time for rearranging chairs, dragging tables across the floor, pounding your keyboard to get the computer working, fiddling with your projector, collating handouts or frantically shuffling through your notes in a last-ditch effort to rehearse.

Jim never believed in the 60/20 Rule. "Why waste time arriving early?"

Own the Room! You are responsible for the success or failure of the session. When the audience arrives, turn your undivided attention to meeting and greeting. Introduce audience members to one another. Be a conversation starter.

You can gather a great deal of valuable and relevant information in 20 minutes. Incorporate this information into your presentation. "Karen, you mentioned prior to our session that you recently had a wonderful customer service experience. Could you share it with everyone?" Karen feels good because you remembered her name, you involved her in the presentation, and she had the opportunity to contribute to the session.

Following the 60/20 Rule will help you appear more prepared. It will also eliminate last minute changes that can cause last minute panic.

Dateline: Palo Alto, California—A corporate real estate broker has a major presentation and is competing with three other companies. As part of the presentation, the broker is planning to use a wireless Internet connection to demonstrate his firm's capabilities.

He is scheduled to deliver his presentation at the prospect's office in a conference room set up for wireless Internet access. The presentation is scheduled for 2:00 p.m., but the broker asks the prospect if he and his team can arrive at noon to set up. He is granted permission to do so. Upon arrival, he finds out that the location for the presentation has been changed. The new venue is not set up for wireless or for any other Internet access. The broker's team spends the next hour figuring out how to connect to the Internet from the conference room.

Arriving two hours early turned out to be a brilliant strategy. The presentation flowed seamlessly. They won the assignment. Reflecting on the sequence of events, the partner leading the team, said, "Can you imagine if we had showed up 20 minutes before our presentation? The Internet portion of the presentation would have been a non-event. We would have had to change—on the fly—everything that we had practiced."

Technology breakdowns can happen to the most tech-savvy presenters. As Bill Gates introduced Windows 98, his computer shut down. He had nothing but a blank screen and a roomful of people scrambling to get the computer up and running again. If it can happen to Bill Gates, it will probably happen to us at some point.

These stories raise important points about the use of technology in a presentation. Technology continues to advance and play a changing role in presentations. In the good old days the only concern was whether the bulb in the overhead projector was going to burn out during the presentation. As technology progressed, there were three concerns: Will the computer shut down on me? Will my slide deck flow as planned? And will the bulb in the projector burn out during the presentation? Fast forward to today. Add to your tool box the use of memory sticks, Web-based conferencing, interactive whiteboards, Internet access, streaming media, and wireless connections. The bulb is the least of your worries. All of these new tools can add impact to a presentation. They can also increase the risk of a technology failure. It used to be that you would load up your car for a presentation with your computer, a couple of easels, some markers and a handout. It's getting to the point where you need to add the Chairman of the Federal Communications Commission to your list of take-alongs.

The question for every presenter then becomes: Is the technology making my presentation significantly better, or is it throwing me off my game?

One disastrous mistake people make is going into a presentation completely dependent on PowerPoint or other tech devices to carry the presentation. Technological aids should be used to enhance the presentation. They should not BE the presentation.

If you can't deliver a presentation without the use of technology, you probably don't know your material well enough.

Preparation is critical in staving off the unexpected. This is especially true when using technology as part of your presentation. I'm not talking about preparing by having your team sit at a conference table, brainstorming about what each team member plans to cover and estimating how long each person will speak. I'm talking about literally walking through the presentation as it will be delivered in front of the live audience, including practicing the use of visual aids and practicing for the occurrence of a technology meltdown.

Bring backup. Know what information can be shared via a flip chart or dry erase board. Place some of your critical information on form boards that you can carry into the room. When a tech snafu happens, a dynamic presenter will use movement, gestures and props to illustrate key concepts. A presentation without the benefit of technology and visual aids requires more participation and interaction with the audience to keep everyone focused. Get your audience more involved. Ask them questions. Elicit comments and opinions.

If the technology breaks down during the presentation, you need to determine if the time it takes to reboot or revive the computer or projector is worth the distraction that will result by delaying the presentation. One can quickly lose momentum and lose the audience while fidgeting and fighting with tech gadgets. Some audiences will commiserate with you. Others don't have time to wait. Know your audience.

>> Even thirty seconds of downtime can kill a presentation.

PRESENTATION PREP SHEET

Presentation to: _____

Date: _____   Time: _____

What is the most important thing for your audience to remember?

_____

_____

_____

Structuring Your Presentation

My objective (Mission, Purpose, Goal) is:

_____

_____

_____

We are positioned as follows or the situation is as follows:

_____

_____

_____

**Ask if your understanding of the situation is correct.

The end result (Benefits, Consequences):

_____

_____

_____

Next step:

_____

_____

_____

Close with your Purpose Statement—"As you leave, I would like you to remember . . .

_____

_____

_____

OUTLINE

Opening–Objective: _____

_____

Body of Presentation

Point #1:
Support:

Point #2:
Support:

Point #3:
Support:

Summary: _____

_____

_____

_____

Purpose Statement: _____

_____

Helpful Info to Review

Who will lead the presentation? _____

What are the roles of team members? _____

_____

_____

_____

Who will attend? _____

A/V requirements: _____

Handouts: _____

Stories/Anecdotes: _____

Contact name and number: _____

CHAPTER FIVE
PASSIONATE

"The orator is the embodiment of the passions of the multitude. Before he can inspire them with any emotion he must be swayed by it himself. Before he can move their tears his own must flow. To convince them he must himself believe."

—Sir Winston Churchill

EXCEPTIONAL PRESENTERS RADIATE PASSION, conviction and enthusiasm. I frequently survey business professionals and ask them to list the characteristics of exceptional presenters. Passionate is the #1 response.

If you don't look and sound passionate about your topic, why would your audience be passionate about your topic?

Feeling passionate is one thing. Looking and sounding passionate is quite another. Our body language, facial expressions, movement, gestures and voice are the implements that convert words into action and transform the printed text into emotion and enthusiasm.

Passionate presenters are more persuasive.

If you want your audience to take action, it is not enough to convince them of your position. They can be convinced, but continue to do nothing. It's more important to persuade them to take action.

Passion is expressed almost entirely through delivery. We can take a passionate, heartfelt, moving speech and turn it into a sleeper by delivering that speech in a monotone, uninspired fashion.

Take the speech by Martin Luther King, Jr., delivered on the steps of the Lincoln Memorial on August 28, 1963. He spoke to over a quarter of a million people. The spirit of his "I have a dream" speech and the words he spoke still resonate in the hearts and minds of Americans everywhere. His speech was passion personified.

Imagine taking Dr. King's script and asking former Federal Reserve Chairman Alan Greenspan to deliver the speech. The impact would be quite different.

There is no one style for passion. It shows up in different delivery styles. Oprah Winfrey demonstrates open, engaging passion. Donald Trump exudes an intense, straightforward passion. Regis Philbin unleashes an exuberant and spirited passion.

Because passion is expressed through our delivery, we will focus our attention on the following skill sets:

- Posture
- Gestures and movement
- Voice command
- Elimination of hesitation and verbal graffiti

"Nothing great can be achieved without enthusiasm."

—Ralph Waldo Emerson

THE POWER OF NON-VERBAL COMMUNICATION

Your non-verbal messages will override anything you say. If you say, "I'm confident that we'll complete the project on time and on budget," but you are backpedaling and looking at your shoes when you say it, the audience will believe your body language. Your words are undermined by your retreating body language. Your words and your non-verbal messages must be congruent.

POSTURE

Our posture and non-verbal communication (eye contact, facial expressions, appearance, movement, body language and gestures) play a major role in our ability to communicate passionately.

Daniel Benjamin, an assistant professor at Cornell University, and Jesse M. Shapiro, from The University of Chicago School of Business, conducted a 2006 study entitled, "Thin-Slice Forecasts of Gubernatorial Elections." Participants in the study watched 10-second silent video clips of competing candidates. "People could predict remarkably well who actually won the election after watching a 10-second silent video of each candidate," says Benjamin. "Because there was no sound, the participants' forecasts were based purely on the candidates' appearance and non-verbal behavior."

What impression do you make on others in the first 10 seconds of visual contact? People begin judging you the instant they establish visual contact. What do they see that enables them to judge you so quickly? Do they see you as a winner? Their judgments are based, to a great extent, on your appearance, posture, movement, facial expressions, eye contact and how you carry yourself.

>> First impressions last.

How do you carry yourself? Do you stand straight, or do you slouch? Do you exude confidence, or do you exude apathy? Do you move with purpose, or do you drag yourself from place to place?

Posture and carriage are excellent indicators of one's confidence, comfort level, experience and attitude. In many cases, posture is our first line of communication.

> **Situation**—You're attending a networking function. You glance at the door as person A enters the room. You know nothing about this person, but your immediate evaluation is that she is confident, professional and credible. You sense that this would be a good person to meet. She has an aura about her.

What visual clues led to those conclusions?

_____

_____

_____

Here are some of the clues you might have picked up on:

- She stood tall and attentive.
- She moved with purpose, keeping her head and eyes up.
- She appeared comfortable making eye contact, even if she didn't know the other person.
- She smiled easily and was quick to offer a handshake.
- You could almost see her energy being transferred to others, and her openness revealed her enthusiasm for the event.

At the same function you see person B. It's easy to see that he had absolutely no interest in attending the function. You sensed that he also had no interest in the people attending the function.

What visual clues led to your conclusions about person B?

_____

_____

_____

Here are some of the clues you might have picked up on:

- He slouched.
- His head and eyes remained down for the most part.
- He would look up long enough to find a familiar face. If he didn't spot a familiar face, his eyes would dart back to the floor.
- His face was expressionless.
- He glanced at his watch several times.
- He labored from one spot to the next.
- He offered no handshakes or greetings.

- His first stop was to the cash bar for a shot of liquid personality.

Think about how this relates to your presentation efforts. Do you tend to get off to a slow start with your audience? Do you have trouble getting the audience to warm up to you? It could be your content or the way you deliver your content. But as it relates to first impressions and non-verbal communication, it could be what your audience observes about you prior to the start of your presentation. Does the audience see a presenter who is open, relaxed, and prepared, or do they see someone who seems distant, nervous and disorganized? Nine out of ten times listening to the presentation of an open, relaxed and prepared presenter will be more enjoyable than attending a session presented by a distant, nervous and disorganized presenter.

>> The tone of the presentation is set before the presentation begins.

If we are aware of our non-verbal communication, then we will be able to make a positive first impression every time. We simply need to be aware of the messages we're sending and adjust our non-verbals accordingly.

As presenters we begin making impressions before we open our mouths to speak. Before we utter our first word, our presence has spoken volumes. We expose our personalities in the way we carry ourselves, in our attire and outward attitude.

"The eyes are more exact witnesses than the ears."

—Heraclitus, Greek philosopher

WHAT IS AN EFFECTIVE BASE POSTURE WHEN STANDING?

Exercise:

When you are in a position to move about safely, stand up and stretch your arms to the side. Stretch your arms up. Reach for the sky. Now, for 30 seconds, close your eyes and completely relax your arms, shoulders, hands and forearms. Relax your head and neck.

When you were completely relaxed, where were your hands? Chances are, your hands were at your sides.

When I conduct this exercise at the beginning of seminars, 99% of the people in the room assume the "relaxed" position, their hands and arms resting at their sides.

Hands down:

- Relaxed
- Confident
- Open

"Hands at the sides" is an excellent base position. Remaining in that position for extended periods would cause a person to look stiff. But as a base position, between gestures and movements, it creates a strong, relaxed presence and helps eliminate distracting and fidgety hand movements.

With your hands at your sides, you appear open, eager, confident and seasoned. You do not appear defensive or like you are trying to hide something.

Occasionally, police officers will attend my workshops. Some have told me that they are trained to approach potentially confrontational situations with their hands at their sides. They want to appear in complete command of the situation. They can't afford to appear hesitant, diffident or threatening.

Exercise:

Suppose your team is running behind schedule on a key project. You deliver the following statement to them. "Ladies and Gentlemen, we must work together and we must find the solution quickly. Otherwise we will lose this customer. (Dramatic pause) Losing this customer is not an option." On the facing page, circle the posture that would create the maximum impact for your message to your team. X out the posture that would create the least impact.

Standing with your hands at your sides takes no effort. You are built to stand that way. Your wrists, arms and shoulder muscles are relaxed. You look relaxed even when you are nervous.

When you are not using your hands to gesture, keep them at your sides.

THE MOST COMMON PRESENTATION POSTURE: T-REX

The most common posture presenters assume is what I call the T-Rex position. Picture a Tyrannosaurus Rex with those tiny arms dangling in front of its massive body. The arms don't appear to have a purpose. They just hang there. Presenters frequently assume the T-Rex position. The hands just dangle in front of the body. I'm sure you've seen it many times. The presenter's arms are locked. As the mouth moves, so do the hands. The hands flail in a futile attempt to participate. The hands appear completely out-of-sync with the message. At times, the hands and mouth appear to be delivering different speeches. If you are in a position to do so safely, assume the T-Rex position. Standing or sitting, it doesn't matter. Join me and engage in some of the distracting activities that occur as a result of T-Rex. See how these feel. You have probably already engaged in several of these activities:

- The "spider on the mirror." Fingertips touching fingertips.
- The "sisters of mercy." Hands in the praying position.
- The "fire starter." Rubbing the hands together in a furious attempt to ignite the brain.
- The "ring leader." Twirling, twisting and tugging the ring.
- The "hand washer." Scrub up.
- "The cuff tugger." Can't get those cuffs out far enough.

Locked in the T-Rex position, presenters unknowingly perform world-class baton twirling routines with pens. They click dry erase markers repeatedly, without a clue that each click sounds to the audience like a shotgun blast. They leaf through notes and turn paper into telescopes. They straighten and reshape paper clips. They check the position of their tie, multiple times. They even clean their fingernails.

By avoiding the T-Rex position you will immediately eliminate numerous distracting idiosyncrasies.

OTHER SPEAKER POSITIONS AND THE MESSAGES THEY SEND:

Fig Leaf

Timid, pensive, inexperienced, feeling vulnerable

Hands in Pockets

Nonchalant, passive, over-confident

Parade Rest

Sheepish, withholding info, hiding something

Hands on Hips

Challenging, defiant, overbearing

"You gotta problem with that?"

"We'd better buckle down."

Arms Crossed

Closed off, restrained

"I'm not buying what you're saying."

WHAT IS THE MOST EFFECTIVE SEATED POSITION?

People tend to get lazy or lax at meetings in which everyone is seated. Be comfortable, but don't be lazy. Don't slouch in your chair. Don't rest your head in your hands.

Keep your hands on the table.

Ann Marie Sabath, a leading expert on business etiquette and author of the book, *One Minute Manners: Quick Solutions to the Most Awkward Situations You'll Ever Face at Work,* recommends that when dining with international clients, we should keep our hands on the table. After all, internationally it is considered a major faux pas when even one hand is not showing. Besides projecting global body language, on the domestic front you will look more engaged in the discussion and perhaps be perceived as more interested in what others have to say.

Ann Marie's advice about using your hands during Power Lunches and other business meals also applies when conducting business at a conference table or desk. Hands above-board! As Sabath says, "If you are interested, others will see you as more interesting."

Later in this chapter we will review the use of gestures to make your presentations more energetic, more vivid and more engaging. As you read about gestures, think of how you can apply them when you are sitting. Apply the same descriptive and well-defined gestures seated as you do standing.

If you are seated in an open area or at a conference table, be aware of the non-verbal messages your posture is sending. Assume an attentive but not rigid posture. Leaning forward will add energy to your delivery. You will appear to have greater enthusiasm for the topic.

When seated at a table or desk, most of your forearms should be on the table. But remember what your mom always told you, "Keep your elbows off the table." The same "elbows off" rule applies when you are presenting.

When seated, keep your hands at least eight to ten inches into the table when gesturing. Hands on the edge of the table look like puppets. It also makes you look tentative.

SQUARE UP

An excellent way to personalize your message is to square your shoulders to the person with whom you are making eye contact. Most presenters only move their head from side to side when making eye contact. Squaring your shoulders invites each person into the presentation.

Squaring up also helps to stabilize your feet and keeps you from drifting, shuffling and swaying.

If you are presenting to a large audience, square up to people in different parts of the room. Remember to square up to the people all the way to your right and left. Draw them into your presentation. You should also do this when presenting from behind a lectern.

It is difficult to ignore someone who is squared up to you and looking you directly in the eye. It feels personal and conversational.

When seated at a conference table, you can still square your shoulders to various audience members. Don't swivel your chair each time you redirect your eye contact to someone new. Rather, during your presentation, randomly square up and establish eye contact.

PRESENTING FROM BEHIND A LECTERN

Here are a few techniques to use when presenting from behind a lectern.

Anything you stand behind during a presentation can act as a barrier between you and your audience. If forced to speak from a lectern, make a special effort to connect.

- Keep your head and eyes up.
- Make eye contact with all parts of the room.

   There is a tendency to focus on the people immediately in front of you. Square your shoulders to the people all the way to your right and to your left. Draw them in. You can accomplish this even when using a microphone.

(*Bulleted list continues on page 70.*)

Using a Microphone

When using a microphone (cordless lapel microphones excluded) remember to ALWAYS project your voice into or through the microphone. This is easy to do when addressing audience members sitting directly in front of you.

When addressing audience members to the left or right, don't forget to speak through the microphone. This is especially true when speaking at a dais with invited guests seated on both sides of the lectern.

Here are two simple microphone rules to ensure your audience hears everything you say:

1. Never speak while your face is turned away from the microphone. Don't let your voice disappear into the abyss of a large ballroom.

2. When making eye contact with people to your right, for example, maintain eye contact with and square your shoulders toward those people. As you do this, lean forward and to your left. By doing so, you maintain eye contact and your voice projects through the microphone.

By following these two simple techniques, you will avoid the "turning away from the microphone" scenario that occurs countless times at banquets and award ceremonies.

Violate the microphone rules and you have this scenario: The master of ceremonies is introducing the Person of the Year. "Ladies and Gentlemen, our Person of the Year has given countless hours of service to this foundation over the last 27 years. She has made the foundation what it is today. No one has contributed more to our success than this year's Person of the Year, Ms. _____. Let's give her a tremendous round of applause. And she's here with her husband, _____.

- Your stomach and the lectern should not meet, especially when using notes or a script.

  If your stomach is against the lectern and your notes are at the bottom edge of the lectern, your face will disappear from the view of the audience every time you glance down at your notes. Slide your notes toward the front of the lectern. Depending on the incline of the lectern, you might need to hold them in place with one hand.

  Move back four to six inches away from the lectern. Now you are in a position to glance at your notes without moving your head. Only your eyes move. Your head stays up. This helps you to appear less dependent on your notes. The people in the back half of the room will not be able to tell whether you are looking at your notes or the people in the front rows.

- Use your hands freely to gesture. Gesture just as you would if there were no lectern in front of you.

- Stand tall. The lectern is a barrier between you and the audience. Make yourself as visible as possible. Many hotels and conference centers have stools that one can stand on when speaking at a lectern. Don't hesitate to ask for a stool if the height or size of the lectern is inhibiting your ability to see and be seen.

- Rest your hands on the lectern. Avoid grabbing the outside edges.

- Don't lean on or hang over the lectern. You will appear tired or lackadaisical. For most audiences, this position is too casual.

- Practice using various note holders to determine what works best for you (5 × 7 cards, three-ring binder, flip pad . . .).

FIDGETY HANDS

Fidgety hands tend to make us appear uncomfortable. In his book, *Telling Lies*, author Paul Ekman writes that his research shows that fidgety hands often reflect a level of discomfort. The perception of someone viewing a fidgety communicator is that the communicator is nervous, uncomfortable with the topic or distorting or avoiding the truth. The more manipulators (rubbing, scratching, touching, or fidgeting) a viewer sees, according to Ekman, the less the viewer tends to trust the information coming from the person using the manipulators.

If you want to build greater credibility with your audience, eliminate fidgety movements and nervous-looking activity.

CAN YOU HANDLE THE PRESSURE?

Under pressure, our bodies seek to be comfortable. We can physically retreat without even realizing it.

- Head and eyes lowering
- Hands diving into the pockets
- Clasping hands behind the back
- Eyes darting to the ceiling or floor
- Backpedaling
- Grappling hands
- Fidgeting with pens, markers or notes
- Hemming and hawing
- Grabbing the back of a chair for support
- Fingers dancing on the table

- Using verbal graffiti, such as "um" and "uh"

FIVE TIPS TO APPEAR RELAXED, CONFIDENT AND PROFESSIONAL

1. Stand tall—don't sway, rock, shuffle or lean.
2. Keep your head and eyes up. Connect with your audience.
3. Smile. A sincere smile warms up the coldest situations.
4. Never retreat.
5. Move with purpose, energy, and enthusiasm.

PRACTICING TO SOLIDIFY EXCEPTIONAL POSTURE

For the next 30 days:

- Practice every time you stand up. Put your hands at your sides.
- Practice the hands down position in every conversation.
- Practice whenever you are standing in line.
- Practice by noticing where others place their hands, especially when under pressure.
- If you have a habit of fidgeting with your hands, keep your hands apart even when you are sitting down. Fidgeting with your hands while seated reinforces a bad habit and makes it more difficult to relax the hands when you are standing.

If you practice your posture for the next 30 days, the hands down position should become your most comfortable position. You should prefer the hands down position to all others (fig leaf, hands in pockets, parade rest, hands on hips or T-Rex).

GESTURES

A study by Jana Iverson, University of Missouri Psychologist, concluded that moving our hands when we speak is innate. She said, "We're born with a propensity to move our hands when we speak."

Iverson's study included the use of gestures by blind children. Blind children will routinely gesture when describing objects, even when they're describing the objects to other blind children. Her conclusion was that gestures are very closely linked to the way we communicate and express ourselves.

A study conducted at the Columbia University revealed that gestures are our way of expressing ourselves and being understood. We use gestures as cues to trigger our recollection.

If you are going to use your hands to gesture, be specific.

There is a tendency for presenters to do one of two things with their hands: 1) restrict their movement in an attempt not to flail, or 2) flail.

Conduct your own study:

- Notice how your hands move when you're talking with close friends or family members.
- Notice your hands when you're giving someone driving directions.
- Notice your hands when you're determined to move someone to your point of view.

- Notice how defined your movements become when you are in a heated argument.
- Notice how other people use their hands while speaking.
- Notice your hands while you are talking on the telephone.

It's no wonder some states have outlawed the use of cell phones while driving. The driver is talking and gesturing wildly with both hands, leaving only the knees to steer the vehicle.

What you will notice is that you use your hands quite freely and expressively. It is hard to restrict the use of our hands when we are excited, angry, adamant or determined. Typically, the more animated we become, the more specific and defined our gestures become.

A University of Texas study found that people remember more of what they see than what they hear. Think of your gestures as traveling visual aids.

Use gestures to bring an additional visual dimension to your presentation. Gestures will boost the amount of information your audience retains.

Almost anything you can design in a computer-generated visual, you can describe using gestures.

FIVE EFFECTIVE WAYS TO INCORPORATE GESTURES

1. Use "The Claw," Your Most Versatile Gesture

The "claw" can and should be used often. It reflects an image of a seasoned professional. It can be used standing or seated, behind a lectern or behind a desk.

At the flip chart, dry erase board and screen, the claw enables a presenter to maintain eye contact with and keep her shoulders square to the entire audience.

Watch *The Weather Channel.* The meteorologists do an excellent job of using the claw at the screen while keeping their shoulders square to the camera.

When To Use The Claw

"We can eliminate that possibility right now."

"Let's set that issue aside for the time being."

"Our competitors will not guarantee their results."

2. When Using Numbers

Use the numbers one through five. Stop at five.

"If you remember only one thing this afternoon . . ."

"The two primary concerns I have are . . ."

"We have three objectives this afternoon."

"The client wants this completed in four days."

"There are five reasons this election is critical."

3. When Using Comparisons

Comparative gestures are best if they mimic the information as it would be illustrated on a slide. Dollar amounts, percentages, numbers and revenue are typically depicted using vertical bar charts. Therefore, perform these gestures vertically.

Use horizontal gestures to demonstrate timelines, phases or stages of a project and chronological sequences.

"Revenue increased from $300 million last year to $420 million this year."

"Profits have decreased from 13% to 11%."

"Vacancy rates have risen from 8% to 17%."

"The lead has grown from 4% to 7% since the debate."

"The project will take nine months. In the first two months here is what we need to accomplish."

"Phase one will take thirty days. Phase two will take ninety days."

"We need to expand from our existing 30,000 square feet to 55,000 square feet."

4. When Using Verbs

"Our goal is to increase revenue while we decrease our
inventory."

"We will expand our existing product line."

"We can consolidate those departments."

5. When Pinpointing Dates and When Using Timelines

"The start date is June 6th."

"We will offer the incentives until July 15th."

"Between now and August 15th, this is our
top priority."

VISUAL AIDS

If you are holding a visual aid such as a magazine article, detail aid or brochure, use it assertively. Position it so that you maintain as much eye contact as possible.

Less Effective

Head down + eyes down = Disengaged

More Effective

Head up + eyes up = Fully engaged

PRACTICE OPPORTUNITIES ABOUND

Well-defined gestures must become second nature, or they can appear ill timed and forced.

- Use crisp, specific gestures in every conversation.
- Practice while you are on the phone. The more defined your movements, the stronger and more direct your voice will sound.
- Volunteer to give directions to anyone who looks lost.
- Purchase an American Sign Language dictionary. Many of the signs are common gestures.
- If asked how many sugars you want in your coffee, don't just tell them "two." Tell them and show them.
- If someone comments on your beautiful wall paper, give them a step-by-step, gesture-filled review of how you measured the area, cut the paper, dunked it in the water, unraveled it and carefully matched up the strips. (You are probably visualizing someone wallpapering as you read this.)

Gestures become second nature through repetition. You cannot become proficient using them only once in a while. The more you gesture in casual conversations, the less you'll have to think about them when you're presenting.

Do not think about your gestures during your presentation. It will only serve to throw you off track. Limit your gestures when reading a scripted presentation. It looks forced.

GESTURES IN SUMMARY

- NO T-REX.
- Get your elbows away from your ribcage.

- As a general rule, keep your gestures below your shoulders and above your waist.
- Use your hands freely.
- Think of gestures as your traveling visual aids.
- Be specific, be specific, be specific. The more defined you look, the more defined your message appears to your audience.
- Don't rush. Fast gestures are ineffective. They resemble flailing hands. Hold your gestures for 2-3 seconds.
- After gesturing, place your hands back at your sides.
- Use both hands. There is a tendency for right-handers to make all right-handed gestures. Left-handers, same thing. Continually using the same hand looks repetitive.
- Avoid the bungee effect where it looks like your hands are tied together with a bungee cord. Where one hand goes,

the other follows. Use one-handed gestures in addition to two-handed gestures. One-handed gestures get your point across with less movement.

>> Don't make gestures the focal point of the presentation. Use gestures to help the audience understand and remember your message.

THE DYNAMICS OF VOICE

If you don't sound interested, why should I be interested?

Ed has taken his voice projection to a whole new level.

Use arrows to match the names with the voice description.
Names can have more than one description.

Passionate	Ronald Reagan	Monotone
Dynamic	Bill Clinton	Stiff/scripted
	Barbara Walters	
Inspirational	Oprah Winfrey	Dry
Enthusiastic	John F. Kennedy	Boring
	Martin Luther King	
Commanding	Donald Trump	Flat
Conversational	Katie Couric	Weak
Lively	Suzie Orman	Uninspired
	Jesse Jackson	
Fun	Dick Vitale	Sing-songy
Friendly	Hillary Clinton	Dull
Interesting	Jon Stewart	Inaudible
	Norman Schwarzkopf	
Spellbinding	Jane Pauley	Lazy
Appealing	Paul Harvey	Irritating
	Regis Philbin	
Intense	Joel Osteen	Tired
Confident	Your voice?	Listless

Did your arrows tend to point in the same direction?
Who do you know who fits the descriptions on the right?
Your voice is an outward expression of your passion. Your voice
can add energy, animation and excitement to your presentation.

VOLUME

People associate a strong voice with confidence. People associate a weak voice with a lack of confidence. Develop a strong, confident voice. Don't scream. Don't yell. Just SPEAK UP.

Most people do not come close to tapping the full potential of their voice. The voice is a valuable tool to becoming an exceptional presenter.

Very few people have recorded themselves delivering a presentation. As a result, they have no way of knowing how their voices sound. The only way to improve the quality of your voice is to know what others are hearing when you speak.

When we get nervous, we tend to speed up our delivery. The more we speed up, the less we breathe. We find ourselves speaking from the throat, instead of allowing our diaphragm and lungs to help boost our decibel level. Speaking from the top of the throat results in a thinner, softer voice.

It can be difficult for soft-spoken people to elevate their volume to an effective level. If one's voice is soft, doubling the volume is barely noticeable to the listeners, but it sounds like shouting to the speaker. People should not have to strain to hear your message. If you speak after taking a breath, you will create more volume and resonance with less effort.

INFLECTION

A dynamic voice tends to be more interesting and engaging than a voice with a narrow range of inflection. Rule of thumb: A dynamic voice reflects passion, excitement, enthusiasm, confidence and commitment

Call a friend at work. You can guess her mood by the tone in her voice when she answers the phone. You can hear her attitude.

Expand the range of your voice. A monotone voice will significantly shorten the attention span of your audience.

PACING/TEMPO

SPEAK, PAUSE, BREATHE, SPEAK

Listen to exceptional communicators. They take their time. They articulate their thoughts. They don't rush. By pausing and breathing, they are able to make words, phrases, numbers and statistics stand out.

People do not hang on every word we say. That is why we need to be deliberate. Use pace and inflection to make your words jump out at your audience. Force the listener to hear what is important for them to hear.

Practice Tapping Your Full Voice Potential

Once you expand the range of your voice, monotone will no longer be acceptable. Your voice will only improve with practice. There are many opportunities during your daily routines to practice the volume, inflection and pace of your vocal delivery.

- Record yourself on a recorder or video camera. Listen to the recording and objectively evaluate your vocal quality, your tone, your energy level, your pace, and your verbal graffiti. Make the adjustments you feel are appropriate.

If you have not heard your recorded voice, let me warn you that it can be an uncomfortable exercise. We are used to hearing our voice from one perspective. Listening to our voice from an outside source will sound different, but that is the voice that other people hear.

Work to make your voice an asset, a vehicle to transport your message.

- Practice every time you leave a voice mail message. Check each message before sending it.

- Practice by reading out loud. Read your favorite morning periodical out loud at the breakfast table. Or close your office door and read aloud as if your voice was being broadcast to listeners all around the country.

- Read children's books to your kids. Use different voices to represent the various characters.

- Mimic radio commercials and disk jockeys. Radio commercials are fast and at the high end of the energy level. They are good for stretching your comfort level. The goal is not to have everyone sound like Dick Vitale. The goal is to encourage you to use your full voice potential.

- Read billboards out loud.

- Notice your voice when you are having a lively conversation with friends or family members. Is it more animated than your presentation voice? It shouldn't be.

- Mimic the voices of politicians and celebrities. Try these: Bill Clinton, George W. Bush, Barbara Walters, Donald Trump, Diane Sawyer, and Jay Leno.

Your voice should bring energy, excitement and enthusiasm to your presentation.

Think about your voice as one of the three presentation dimensions. The other two are content and physical delivery. It will behoove you to tap your full voice potential. Your voice is too valuable of a tool not to maximize its impact.

Don't be monotone.

Be dynamic!

ELIMINATE VERBAL GRAFFITI

Call it verbal graffiti, call it trash, call it filler, call it padding. Call it anything you want, but be sure to call it "unprofessional." Most importantly, eliminate it from your vocabulary.

Clearly, filler um adds like nothing to our effectiveness, you know what I mean? Um, basically it like dilutes the impact of our um message, OK? And, to be honest with you (I've been lying to you up until now), it causes us, you know, to sound um unprepared and um unprofessional, see?

Some will argue that filler is conversational. They contend that filler is natural and does not impact the message. I vehemently disagree.

Has the President of the United States ever written filler into a State of the Union address or Inaugural speech? The answer is "no." If filler was natural, you would think the President would direct his speechwriters to "Throw in a dozen or so 'ums' and six or seven 'you knows.'"

Martin Luther King did not use filler in his impassioned "I have a dream" speech. It wasn't the "I have a um, you know, like a dream" speech.

In an Inaugural speech that inspired mankind to put a man on the moon, John F. Kennedy did not say, "To be honest with you, fellow Americans, we um basically choose to, you know, put a man on the uh moon."

The filler phrase I get the biggest kick out of is, "To be honest with you." Have you been lying to me up until now? Three minutes later the person will say, "To be perfectly honest with you." I see, you were being honest before, now you're really going to be honest.

Television sit-com characters rarely use filler unless the character is supposed to appear uninformed, uneducated or confused.

Dateline: Philadelphia—A design firm founder receives a call from an existing client. The client compliments the founder on the work his firm is providing, but indicates that one matter needs attention. The client asks that the partner leading the assignment no longer be allowed to present to the client. Although the partner is quite competent in his work, his "ums" and "uhs" are quite distracting. The client states that this partner uses so much filler that, "We can't stand it any more." During a recent conference call, the client had someone count the number of "ums" and "uhs" used during the call. The partner averaged 26 "ums" or "uhs" per minute during the call.

This is probably the most remarkable verbal graffiti story I have ever heard. The client feels that the partner is doing great work, but they don't want to hear from him any more. "Keep him on our assignment, but have someone else communicate with us."

Practice Techniques for Eliminating Verbal Graffiti

Practice every day until filler is no longer a part of your working vocabulary. From this point forward:

- Do not use filler while leaving voice mail messages. Listen to your outgoing voice mail before hitting the send button.
- Notice how much filler other people use in voice mail messages. Does it sound professional?
- Eliminate filler in casual conversations.
- Record yourself during phone conversations (you don't need to record both sides of the conversation). Listen for filler. Try to determine your filler patterns.

You will soon be able to anticipate your filler. If you can anticipate it, you can eliminate it.

Filler can become engrained in your vocabulary. It will most likely take two to four months to eliminate your existing filler. How long it takes will depend entirely on your determination. If you want it out, you can get it out.

Other commonly used graffiti, filler and non-words:

We **clearly** must move on this. It is **clearly** . . .

We **actually** have a process and it **actually** works. **Frankly** I'm not concerned. I **frankly** think we should . . .

We will proceed cautiously, **and so on and so forth.**

To be honest, I don't know.

Well, there you go again.

Like I said before, we're working on it.

I mean, they took the contract and, **I mean**, tore it up.

Qualifiers

Words that dilute your impact and sound timid.

I think we need to move on this.	vs	We need to move on this.
I guess it's time to begin.	vs	It's time to begin.
We **kind of** missed the deadline.	vs	We missed the deadline.
I **sort of** secured the account.	vs	I secured the account.
Maybe we should reduce inventory.	vs	We should reduce inventory.

There are times when "I think" and "I guess" are appropriate. Use them sparingly.

BE AWARE OF THE "CONDESCENDORS"

What are they? They are words we add on at the end of statements. We use them to make sure the audience is with us. Used too often, they sound condescending.

You need to sign this by next week, **OK?**

After it's signed, return it to us, **OK?**

If it's approved, we'll move forward, **OK?**

Repeat the sentences replacing **OK** with "**see.**"

Repeat the sentences replacing **see** with "**right.**"

Condescendors leave the impression that the presenter is not confident in the listener's ability to comprehend the information.

What verbal graffiti do you use?

For three days, notice the verbal graffiti you use. Then come back to this page and write your verbal graffiti below.

_____

_____

_____

What verbal graffiti do you notice other people using?

Sit with this book as you watch television interviews. Listen to people who are having casual conversations. What graffiti do you hear? Write the graffiti you notice others using below.

_____

_____

_____

If in three days you have a heightened awareness of verbal graffiti, I'm confident that you will be determined to eliminate yours.

How Do I Eliminate Verbal Graffiti from My Vocabulary?

The use of filler is a habit, just as body language is a habit. How do you change the habit of using verbal graffiti?

Eliminating verbal graffiti is a four-step process:

Step One: **Gain an awareness** of the verbal graffiti you tend to use.

Record yourself and review the recording. Listen to your voice mail messages before sending them. Notice the verbal graffiti you use in casual conversation.

Step Two: **Recognize your pattern.** Some common patterns include:

"Ums" at the beginning of sentences or when transitioning from one thought to another. "Ums" preceding items being listed.

"You know" being used when you are speaking rapidly or speaking off the cuff.

"And" serving as a connector to the next sentence, replacing the period.

"Really" becoming the primary choice to add emphasis to another word. "I really mean it this time."

Ending sentences with, "OK?," "Right?, "See?", or "Know what I'm saying?"

"To be honest with you" when you are trying to be completely open with someone.

Step Three: **Anticipate** that you are about to use verbal graffiti.

Step Four: **Pause.** Resist the urge to fill, and then state your next word. This is the most difficult step.

Verbal graffiti can become so engrained in speech patterns that eliminating them seems to be a monumental task. But doing so is well worth the effort. Having your words flow more clearly and concisely will pay handsome dividends. Your core message will stand out. You will be perceived as more definitive and more intelligent.

Make "eliminate graffiti" a 24/7 project. It will not take long to eliminate the words and non-words that cloud your message.

Now that we've covered the majority of the delivery techniques, use the following observation sheet to analyze a TV guest.

Note: Additional observation sheets are included in the back of the book. I recommend that you fill out one observation sheet per week for the next three weeks to reinforce what you've learned.

OBSERVATION SHEET

We learn a great deal from observing others. Analyze guests being interviewed on TV shows such as *Meet the Press*, *This Week*, *Hardball*, *20/20*, *O'Reilly Factor*, *Crossfire*, and *60 Minutes*.

Show: _____   Date: _____

Guest: _____   Host: _____

Initial impression of guest: _____

Message was: Well defined/diluted/sidetracked

Why: _____

_____

Write the first two words or sounds of the guest's answers:

_____   _____   _____

Physical Presence

Fidgety? If so, how? _____

Were movements and gestures: Defined/limited/nebulous

Adjustments in chair: Frequent/noticeable/infrequent

Posture: Strong/passive/weak. Describe: _____

_____

_____

Eye contact: Sustained/fleeting

Voice: Unwavering/cautious/hesitant

Filler used and frequency: _____

Did content dictate comfort level? _____

If so, how? _____

Rate the effectiveness of the guest
(1 being disastrous and 10 being successful): _____

Overall observations: _____

_____

_____

CHAPTER SIX
ENGAGING: TO EARN THEIR RESPECT, YOU MUST FIRST CONNECT

EXCEPTIONAL PRESENTERS CONNECT with their audiences. They build rapport quickly and involve audiences early and often.

If you fail to show a genuine interest in your audience, why should they be interested in you or your message?

Five surefire ways to alienate yourself from any audience:

1. Talk about yourself.
2. Avoid eye contact.
3. Don't smile.
4. Read your entire speech.
5. Use inappropriate or sarcastic humor.

Don't forget that the average adult undivided attention span is approximately 15-30 seconds. Think about how we watch television. We have the remote control within reach or in hand at all times (partly because we don't want to relinquish control). We continuously flip from channel to channel looking for something that grabs our attention. We stay on that channel only as long as it holds our interest. Then we flip again.

I don't think that we're flipping channels because we get bored. We don't even give ourselves enough time to get bored. What we're watching simply isn't holding our attention.

Picture your audience members holding remote controls in their hands. The remotes are aimed at you, the presenter. If you fail to hold their attention, they are poised and positioned to flip to another channel. Worse yet, they are ready to hit the "off" button.

I used to talk about techniques designed to maintain the attention of your audience. I have since given up on that idea and now focus on how to continually regain the attention of your audience.

RULES OF ENGAGEMENT

Here are 11 ways exceptional presenters connect with their audiences:

1. Speak to the Interests of Your Audience

As the saying goes, "People don't care how much you know, until they know how much you care."

Presenters often make the mistake of talking about what is important to the presenter, not to the audience. Engage your audience by talking about what's important to them.

How do you find out what is important to your audience? You ask. See Chapter Eight, "Understand Your Audience."

It amazes me how many proposals end up being a Niagara Falls of information about the presenter or her company. It's the classic, "Hey, we've been talking about me for the last twenty minutes. What about you? What do you think of me?"

- "I've been in business for 22 years."
  Congratulations, but does that mean I should do business with your competitor because they've been in business 25 years?

- "We have 350 locations worldwide."
  Big deal. What does that mean to my business in South Bend, Indiana? How are your other 349 locations going to help me?

- "I really want your business."
  So does everybody else. Do you expect us to hand you the business just because you want it? What are you going to do to impact my bottom line?

- "Our client list is extensive."
  The firm we just heard from before you showed up had an awesome client list.

- "I've been our number one salesperson for five straight years."
  So what, how much money has that put in my pocket?

Take every piece of information in your presentation and visualize the prospect or client saying "So what? What does that mean to me and my business? How will you add value to my project?"

Know the answers before you present.

2. Use Stories, Examples and Anecdotes

Stories bring presentations to life. They make information relevant to the listener. People tend to remember the story and the message behind the story longer than they remember facts, figures and formulas.

Stories, anecdotes and examples can elicit a range of emotions and reactions from your audience. They create visual images.

Most exceptional presenters have developed their storytelling ability to an enviable plateau. They use stories to stimulate the listeners' minds and to instill their message.

Use stories, examples and anecdotes at the start of your presentation or as a powerful way to end your speech.

3. Eye Contact Is an Essential Engagement Tool

When you meet someone for the first time who will not look you in the eye, what do you tend to think of that person?

- She's insincere.
- He's not interested in me.
- She has low self-esteem.
- I question his knowledge.
- I question her expertise.
- I'm not sure if I can trust him.
- She doesn't like me.
- He's lying.
- She's arrogant.
- He's shy.
- She's preoccupied.

In some cultures eye contact can be perceived as aggressive or disrespectful. Know your audience and adjust your delivery.

Look at your audience! Don't glance and dart around the room. Lock-on for three to four seconds. Allow yourself time to connect. Avoid the "feeding bird syndrome." Watch a bird at a feeder. Its head is constantly whipping around checking for danger. Birds at feeders rarely look relaxed. The same is true with speakers. Their heads move back and forth as if on a swivel. If you sustain eye contact three to four seconds, it helps stabilize your head and also helps stabilize your body.

The Windows to the Presenter's Soul

STUMPED   ROLLING EYES   THINK

I'M NOT SURE   WHAT?   OH YEAH

UM   ENGAGED   NOT AGAIN

Lock-on to One and Connect with Many

If your audience is large, lock-on to individuals in various sections of the room. When you lock-on to one person, there are several others around that person who think you are looking at them as well.

A CEO client and I were talking about Bill Clinton's effectiveness as a presenter. He commented that when Bill Clinton establishes sustained eye contact with one individual, it feels as though he is connecting with many individuals.

Some people are more comfortable looking over the heads of the audience. This technique makes the presenter more comfortable but the audience wonders, "What the heck is he looking at?"

Pretend the person you're making eye contact with is the only person in the room. By doing so, you create a one-on-one feel to your presentation. The person you're looking at feels connected. Your delivery appears personal and conversational.

Be Generous—Share Your Eye Contact with All

A critical, yet common presentation blunder is to look exclusively at the person thought to be the decision-maker. By doing so, the presenter alienates the other people in the room. The nonverbal message says to the audience, "You are not important."

How can we possibly know who makes the final decisions? Do we base it on job titles? Do we base it on who appears to be the most influential? Do we even know the decision-making process?

Even if we're correct in pinpointing the decision-maker, we don't necessarily know who else will influence the decision, or how much influence they have. When we leave the room, the decision-maker might turn to the group and ask, "What do you think?" If we've alienated the group, they will not have positive regards for us. They will have the same feelings about us that we have about people who don't look us in the eye: insincere, not interested, lying, arrogant or low self-esteem.

> **Dateline: Los Angeles**—A top-producing broker delivers a proposal. Her audience: the prospect's CEO, CFO and a Sr.VP. She did not win the business. She later found out that the Sr.VP felt that she had been arrogant, and she probably would not give them the attention they deserved. Reflecting on her meeting, the broker remembered looking at and talking to the CEO and CFO. She did not remember looking at or talking to the Sr.VP. She made the fatal mistake of thinking the CEO and CFO were the final decision-makers. In fact, the Sr.VP played a significant role in the decision. The broker's lack of eye contact with the Sr.VP cost her a large commission and the opportunity to work with a company that will need additional services for years to come.

>> Common sense and common courtesy suggest that we share our eye contact with every person in the room.

Don't Gravitate to the Friendly Faces

It's possible that the unfriendly looking person is preoccupied with an upcoming project deadline. It's possible that they had a fight with their spouse earlier in the day. They could have been up all night with a sick child.

It's interesting that the person who looks least interested during a session will be the first to come up afterward and say how much she enjoyed the session. Makes me wonder what she looks like when she doesn't enjoy a session.

As you continue to share your eye contact with members of the audience, interesting conversions will take place. Audience members who refused to make eye contact early in the presentation will suddenly make sustained eye contact. People who had that, "I couldn't be more bored" look will suddenly look interested.

Position Yourself So That You Are the Focus of Attention

Because our eyes are drawn to movement, a conference room with a glass wall can be the kiss of death for a presentation. If your audience is facing the glass, you can be assured that they will look at every person who walks past the glass. The same person will walk by seven times, and everyone will glance at her every time. Position yourself so that you and your visual aids are the focus of attention.

Practicing Eye Contact

Eye contact is the easiest of the skills to practice.

- Practice in every conversation. Lock-on for three to four seconds.
- Make note of who you tend to look at while presenting.
- Make note of where your eyes wander when you're not interested, when you disagree, when you're angry or when you're scrambling to respond to a question.

- When the pressure is on, hang tough. Don't break eye contact. Fleeing eyes reflect uncertainty and insecurity.

- Observe others under pressure. Watch their eyes. Do their eyes dart to the ceiling or to the floor? Do you sense poise or panic in their eyes?

- When conversing with a group at a business or networking function, share your eye contact with everyone.

- Practice with every handshake. Lock eyes. Be present and fully engaged.

- Practice by giving others your undivided attention.

Develop a high level of comfort with eye contact. It is an essential tool to engaging your audience.

4. Don't Waste Time Talking to Inanimate Objects

Fact: No screen, flip chart, dry erase board, floor, ceiling or conference table has ever, I repeat, ever made a decision.

Pay close attention to how much time you spend looking at a screen or flip chart, a detail aid or sample product. Minimize your eye contact with the OBJECT. Maximize your eye contact with the PEOPLE in the room.

Keep Your Shoulders Square to the Audience

Presenters who are using computer generated visuals, flip charts, or dry erase boards tend to repeatedly glance at their visuals. Presenters can eat up chunks of time looking at their slides instead of looking at their audience. And the more presenters look at their visuals, the less familiar they appear with their material.

Less
effective

More
effective

5. Smile

A smile eases tension and creates a warm environment. A smile lights up one's eyes. A smile says, "I've done this before, I'm confident and I'll do my best to make this an interesting and informative session."

A smile indicates that you are:

- Relaxed.
- Confident.
- Approachable.
- Prepared.

Nervous people tend not to smile. People who are preoccupied or unprepared tend not to smile.

Don't hold your smile back. Show some teeth. If you say something that is intended to be funny, enjoy the moment. Keep your head and eyes up. If they laugh or smile, that's wonderful. If they don't, simply move on to your next point.

If you appear relaxed, your audience will relax. Audiences, for the most part, want the presenter to do well. They appreciate the work and preparation a presentation takes. Most people hope the material is interesting and informative. Most people are glad that it's you presenting and not them.

There are times when it is inappropriate to smile. You will most likely recognize these situations.

6. Use Names Early and Often

"Remember that a person's name is to that person the sweetest and most important sound in any language."
—Dale Carnegie

It is important to mingle before meetings in order to meet and greet the audience. Learn their names. Find out their expectations. Introduce people to one another.

Make a Seating Chart

As people walk into the room, shake hands, introduce yourself, chat and then write down their names on your seating chart.

Use the seating chart to write down comments you heard prior to the meeting. Reference those comments during the meeting. If you have forgotten someone's name, ask for it again, "What is your name again?" Then use the name immediately.

Do not use a person's name as you look down at the seating chart. Look at the chart, talk for 5 to 10 seconds and then say,

"Lynn, we discussed this issue prior to the meeting."

The use of names:

- Shows that you care.
- Builds rapport.
- Creates participation.
- Grabs their attention.
- Stops distracting conversations.

7. Get to Your Feet

>> We're more persuasive on our feet than in our seat.

Own the Room is about being in control of what happens during your presentation. Getting to your feet enables you to take charge and control the flow of information. It allows you to change the dynamics of the room, create energy and assume a more commanding posture.

A study at the University of Minnesota concluded that if we stand up and present our information using some kind of visual aid, we are 43% more likely to persuade the listener.

What makes us more persuasive when we stand?

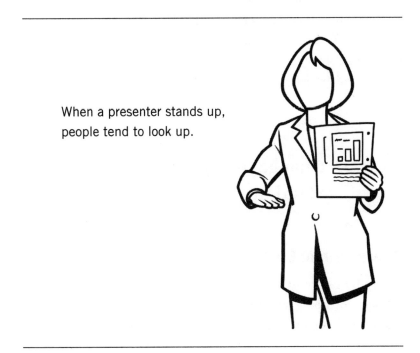

When a presenter stands up, people tend to look up.

- We can make eye contact with everyone in the room.
- We speak from a position of authority and command.
- When a presenter stands up, people tend to look up.
- We can physically move closer to the audience.
- We are more easily seen and heard.
- Voice projection is enhanced.
- We're better able to use visual aids: a flip chart, dry erase board, map, photo, projected image or prop.
- Movement, animation and visuals create energy and lengthen attention spans.
- We can express ourselves more completely.

Eyes are instinctively drawn to movement. To maintain the attention of your audience, MOVE. Don't drift. Move with purpose and make movement meaningful. Create an active environment in which it is easy to pay attention.

It is difficult to pay attention to a one-dimensional presenter. One-dimensional means that the presenter sits down, doesn't use visuals and projects little, if any, animation. Just words, words, words.

>> Change the dynamics of the room.
Stand up.

8. Use Current Events and Periodicals

Incorporate current events or periodicals that tie directly to your message. By doing so, you create the impression that your information is fresh and that you are on top of what is happening in the world. It also demonstrates your effort to bring current and relevant information to your audience.

Speakers who deliver the same speech repeatedly appreciate this technique. Using that day's *New York Times*, for example, sounds fresh. It turns a canned speech into an impromptu speech. The more recent the event or the periodical, the greater the effect.

Use periodicals your audience is likely to be familiar with. Business groups for example relate to periodicals such as the *Wall Street Journal, Forbes, Fortune, Investor's Daily*, or *The Financial Times*.

If you want to grab the attention of an audience of accountants say, "How many of you have seen this month's issue of the *Journal of Accountancy?*" They will be favorably impressed, especially if you are not an accountant.

Magazines and newspaper articles can be a source of humor for your presentation. If you find something in an article to be funny, your audience will likely find it funny as well.

9. Humor

"Against the assault of laughter, nothing can stand."

—Mark Twain

There is nothing like humor to break down barriers, build rapport and disarm opponents. Comedian/pianist Victor Borge once said, "Laughter is the shortest distance between two people."

During the 1984 presidential campaign, questions were raised about the impact of President Reagan's advancing age on his ability to lead. During a debate with Walter Mondale, the President was asked a question about age and the election. President Reagan responded, "I refuse to make age an issue in this election. I will not exploit, for political purposes, my opponent's youth and inexperience."

Walter Mondale joined the audience in a hearty laugh and later admitted that Reagan's humorous response marked the end of any chance he had to win the election. Age took a back seat to other issues from that point forward.

Much has been written about humor through the years. If a proven formula for being funny existed, everyone would have it.

Here are a few tips:

- It is hard to dislike someone with whom you find yourself laughing.

- Stories are better than jokes. Most have probably already heard your joke. It takes a great deal of practice and experience to be an effective joke teller. Tie the story to your message. If no one laughs, your message has still been delivered.

- Keep a journal of events, quotes, stories and situations you find amusing.

- Observe the people with whom you communicate most. What do they find funny?

- Draw from all sources (books, magazines, cartoons, TV, radio and conversations).

Adapt a quote to the occasion.

"I refuse to join any club that would have me as a member."
    —Groucho Marx

"I refuse to live in any country that would elect me to public office."
    —Political advisor James Carville.

Quote Books Cover Virtually Any Topic

"I often quote myself. It adds spice to my conversation."
—George Bernard Shaw

The Forbes Book of Business Quotations

The Reader's Digest Treasury of Modern Quotations

Speaker's Library of Business Stories, Anecdotes and Humor by Joe Griffith

Dictionary of Modern Quotations, J.M. and M.J. Cohen

Using a quote off the cuff demonstrates a quick mind and in many cases, quick wit. Stay alert. Keep a log of quotes that will support your message or make them laugh.

Read Books on Comedy

95 Ways to Use Humor for More Effective Teaching and Training by Doni Tamblyn

Comedy Writing Secrets, 2nd Edition by Mel Helitzer and Mark Shatz

Comedy Writing Step by Step by Gene Perret

Bloopers, Blunders, Jokes, Quips & Quotes by Jim Kraus

There are numerous books filled with serious and humorous quotes from famous people:

The Kennedy Wit, Published by The Citadel Press

The Quotable Reagan by Peter Hannaford

10. Read Your Audience

Marty always amazed himself with his ability to "captivate" an audience.

By now I hope you agree that body language, movement, facial expressions and voice all send messages to your audience. Use your newly acquired knowledge to pick up messages being sent by your audience. Your audience will provide an abundance of feedback IF you watch for the messages they're sending.

A CEO client disclosed to me that since becoming aware of the importance of verbal and non-verbal messages, he pays close attention to the audience as he conducts Q&A sessions. He watches the body language, eye contact and facial expressions of the person asking the question as well as listens for vocal intonation and inflection. He said he can tell from his observations if the questioner is seeking additional information, is confused, is ill-informed, is doubting the information, or is eager to gain additional knowledge.

As he answers a question, he makes it a point to watch the body language and expressions of the audience to evaluate their receptivity to the information.

Presenters who look at the floor, lock onto their notes or haphazardly pan the room miss an abundance of audience feedback. Be alert for the subtle glances, facial expressions, posture and physical reactions.

In an interview with Bryant Gumbel, comedian Jerry Seinfeld said that a comedy routine should be a dialogue rather than a monologue. He has to communicate with the audience even if he is doing all the talking.

People will glance at a decision-maker to see how she reacts to what is being said. Perhaps the presenter has hit on a sensitive issue.

Note the glances, frowns and smirks. Listen for the sighs. They mean something. If you see a reaction that indicates confusion or disagreement, address it. "Is everyone clear on that point?" or "Bill, do you agree with our premise?" or "Cathy, do you have any concerns thus far?"

By doing so, you accomplish three things: 1) you clear up any confusion or misunderstanding, 2) you get the audience involved and allow them to air feelings and comments, and 3) you demonstrate that you are sensitive to the concerns of your audience.

Facial expressions can indicate agreement, disagreement, confusion, exhaustion and other emotions.

Eye contact and attention seem to go hand in hand. If you're losing their eye contact, you're probably losing their attention.

Is their body language open or closed? Are they leaning forward with interest? Are they stretching and yawning? Are they frequently adjusting in their seats, indicating discomfort?

Are they asking questions? Participating? Are they taking notes?

If your audience looks distracted, uninterested, bored, antsy or tired, they probably are. Change topics. Change the tempo. Move to different material. Take a break. Get them to stand and stretch. Ask someone for a comment. Get them involved.

Audiences mentally drift in and out of presentations and conversations all the time. Don't take it as an insult if an audience member seems adrift. Attention spans are brief. It's your responsibility to do everything possible to regain their interest.

When you look at someone in your audience, notice how he may appear to be looking back, but you're quite sure his mind is elsewhere. Seconds after you make eye contact, he shakes his head as if he has been driving a car for too many hours.

At a seminar last year I observed one of those head shakes from a gentleman sitting in the front row. I asked, "Where were you just then, Jeremy?" He answered, "Canoeing." He was going canoeing the following day.

Few, if any, presenters can hold the undivided attention of an audience for extended periods. But it is every presenter's responsibility to use all available tools and techniques to maintain the attention of the audience and make the presentation a productive experience.

Be alert for non-verbal communication from your audience. Although body language is not 100% accurate in predicting what someone is feeling, we should stay alert for the signals. Going the extra mile to engage your audience shows that you care. Listen to the body language of your audience and adjust your message and delivery accordingly.

>> We can't determine the exact thoughts, moods or interests of an audience by watching body language. We can, however, pick up valuable clues as to how the audience feels.

Much has been written about body language. Below, you will find common non-verbal indicators you can use to evaluate, in a non-scientific way, the mood of your audience.

Attentive Audience

Nodding head yes	I agree, I understand
Sustained eye contact	I'm following you
Sitting up/leaning forward	I'm interested, tell me more
Smiling	Engaged, enjoying the info
Laughing at subtle humor	Tuned in
Comments and questions	I want to be involved
Taking notes	Eager to learn and remember
Relaxed posture	Comfortable, open to info

Inattentive or Bored Audience

Sparse eye contact	Interest is waning
Head held up by hands	Bored, tired
Rubbing eyes	Ready to move on
Shifting in seat, fidgeting	Antsy, mentally moving on

Yawns	· · ·	Tired, bored or nervous
Arms and legs crossed	· · ·	Closed off, not buying it
Head and eyes down	· · ·	Mentally somewhere else
Picking lint off clothes	· · ·	This is getting tedious
Eyes wandering around room	· · ·	Tell me something new
Blank stare	· · ·	Daydreaming, adios

General Signs of Nervousness or Discomfort

- Avoiding eye contact
- Clearing throat repeatedly
- Fidgety hands—scratching, playing with pen
- Speaking rapidly
- Sounding winded when speaking
- Perspiration under arms
- Rapid leg bounce
- Chewing objects such as pens, fingers
- Twirling hair
- More hesitation in their speech
- More mispronounced words
- Higher pitched voice
- Voice "cracking"
- Defensive or guarded
- Shifting frequently in their seat
- Awkward or sudden smiles, giggles or laughs

11. Get Your Audience Involved

"I hear and I forget, I see and I remember, I do and I understand."
—Chinese proverb

If you want people to remember your message, get them involved. Encourage participation. If they hear, see and participate in the development of the message, they will certainly walk away retaining much more than if you simply lecture to them.

>> Audience members who expect to participate pay closer attention than those who don't expect to participate.

Techniques for involvement:

- State up front that audience participation is expected.
- Ask them a question and wait for a response.
- Use the phrase, "Write this down" followed by a list.
- Use props: maps, flipcharts, dry erase boards, products, drawings. Set them in various locations in the room. Use these tools to create movement and energy.
- Use an outline that requires the audience to fill in the blanks.
- Distance—get to your feet in order to get closer to the audience. It is difficult to ignore someone who is squared up to you, looking you straight in the eye.
  **Be alert not to violate personal space.

- Use audience members in your stories and examples. This technique not only draws the attention of the person whose name was mentioned but also helps the entire group to refocus.

- Use names. This is another technique to attract the attention of the person named and to help refocus the entire audience.

- Ask their opinion. People generally enjoy sharing opinions with anyone and everyone, even when no one is listening. Be careful not to let this get out of hand. Opinions can sometimes divide groups into packs based on their sensitivity to that topic and can quickly sidetrack the flow of the presentation.

- Conduct a survey.

- Have them raise their hands. "How many of you have ever . . . ?"

- Group discussions and assignments. When using these activities, be sure to monitor the time and work hard to keep the groups focused. If not managed effectively, group work can quickly disintegrate into group gossip and gab sessions.

- Periodicals—share something current and relevant. Don't pass it around lest you will immediately lose their attention.

- Use video clips that match your message. Humorous clips can be especially effective.

- Periodically reward someone for a response or comment.

To Handout or Not to Handout

A never-ending dilemma involves what should be handed out prior to, during or after a presentation. Should we hand out an outline, the slide deck, a list of references, a spreadsheet or an article?

Every presentation is different, and every audience is different. What does the audience expect? What are they used to receiving? (What they are used to receiving does not always dictate what you should hand out.)

Some corporate cultures have strict rules about what can be brought into a presentation, what the handouts should entail and the specific format of the handouts.

"To handout or not to handout" is truly a judgment call on your part. The answer lies in weighing what you gain from handing something to the audience against what you lose by placing something in their hands.

As soon as you hand something to the audience, you immediately lose 50% of their attention. This percentage is not a research-based number, and I would venture to say that in reality you lose a higher percentage than 50%. Generally, the more detailed the handout, the more the attention is drawn to the handout and away from you.

Let's say that you are delivering a presentation to your Board of Directors. Your strategy going into the presentation is to lead the Board members through the outline/slide deck as you demonstrate, page by page, the systematic and logical progression that led to your solution. Your solution will make perfect sense to the Board if you are able to walk them through the process that led to your conclusion.

Before you begin, you circulate copies of your slide deck to the Board members so that they can easily follow along. The reality during the presentation turns out much different than your pre-presentation expectations. You are beginning to explain page two of the handout, but both the CEO and the President have already flipped to the final page in order to get to the bottom line. Your strategy for the flow of the presentation has been derailed.

If you decide to provide a handout and you need the audience to stay with you, you have to pull out all the stops to keep them with you. You simply can't allow them to drift ahead.

Even a concerted effort to hold their attention can fail. Senior level management and bottom line oriented decision makers have a tendency to take the presentation where they want it to go. If they want to jump to your solution, skipping your strategic steps, then chances are you have to jump with them to the solution. This can leave you scrambling to backfill the steps.

If you decide to use a handout remember:

- You immediately lose _____ % (you fill in the number) of the attention of your audience.

- It takes a major effort to keep the audience with you and prevent the audience from flipping ahead.

- If they do flip ahead, be as professional and assertive as you can in the way you lead them back to the page on which you need them to focus.

A handout can be an integral part of any presentation. It can support and even add sizzle to the overall presentation. It can be a tangible reflection of the time, thought and effort you put into the presentation. It can provide the audience a way to follow along and take notes during the presentation. It can visually reinforce your key points.

To handout or not to hand out. The choice is yours.

CHAPTER SEVEN
NATURAL

EXCEPTIONAL PRESENTERS ARE NATURAL. Their style is conversational, and they look completely at ease in front of any audience.

A presentation by a natural presenter sounds lively, it flows easily, and though it is well rehearsed, it does not sound scripted, stiff, stilted, or canned. Natural is making it look like you've done it a 1,000 times before. Natural presenters are fluid, their eye contact is engaging, and their voice is easy to listen to.

By natural, I do not mean someone who was born a naturally exceptional presenter. Exceptional presenters achieve that status by working at it and practicing the art of presenting. In the years I have been coaching, booking and researching speakers, I have yet to come across a single exceptional presenter who said they were exceptional from the beginning.

It is difficult to look and sound natural when you are reading a script. It is difficult, though possible, to sound natural when your speech is memorized. If you rehearse enough times, even a verbatim speech can sound conversational. But how many times are enough? Probably more times than you have time for. It is difficult to look and sound natural when delivering a speech from a teleprompter. President Ronald Reagan was truly talented at the teleprompter. His years as a broadcaster certainly heightened his talent.

Keep in mind that the written word generally does not flow in the same manner as the spoken word. If you do feel compelled to write out your presentations and follow your scripts, try to write them less formally, the way you speak.

Formal scripted:

"Your generous presence at this important gathering of senior-level leaders this evening is gratifying to our entire organization."

Conversational:

"We're grateful that you took the time to clear your busy schedules to be with us this evening."

Having a natural/conversational communication style is especially important when interviewing for a job.

An effective recruiter will try to get a candidate out of her comfort zone to find out who the candidate truly is. Recruiters will routinely work to get past the pre-planned, boilerplate responses candidates have prepared. Some recruiters take a hard-line approach, using rapid fire questions designed to keep the candidate off balance. Others will try to create a more relaxed atmosphere and help the candidate feel at ease, thus uncovering the real person. Still others adjust their tactics based on the position to be filled.

The techniques in this book, once second nature, should benefit any job candidate in the interview process. The techniques help to project a more organized, confident, educated, passionate, engaging, and natural image.

Remember the *Wall Street Journal* corporate recruiters' survey. The hiring attributes listed most often by corporate recruiters were communication and interpersonal skills.

An engaging presenter has the ability to draw the audience in and create a conversational atmosphere. Engaging presenters sound as though they are having a lively conversation with friends instead of sounding scripted, didactic or speechy.

How would you rate the following individuals as it relates to their ability to communicate in a natural manner? Fill in the blanks with the names that you believe fit into each category. Add a few names of your own to the lists.

Natural		Not So Natural
Conversational	Rudy Giuliani	Scripted
Open	Hillary Clinton	Guarded
Engaging	Condoleezza Rice	Distant
Spontaneous	Al Gore	Programmed
Off-the-cuff	Ronald Reagan	Talking points
Quick to respond	John Kerry	Hesitant
Captivating smile	Bill Clinton	Forced smile
Comfortable laugh	Oprah Winfrey	Strained laugh
_____	Tony Blair	_____
_____	Barack Obama	_____
_____	Donald Trump	_____
_____	Tiger Woods	_____
_____	Lance Armstrong	_____

CHAPTER EIGHT
UNDERSTAND YOUR AUDIENCE

"Exchange members must attempt to learn essential facts about every customer and account. General guidelines suggest the registered representative should know each customer's present holdings, financial situation, risk tolerance, needs and objectives."

—New York Stock Exchange Rule 405

STOCKBROKERS ARE REQUIRED TO "KNOW THE CUSTOMER" prior to making any investment recommendations. If they fail to do so, brokers run the risk of fines, loss of license, or worse.

Just as stockbrokers must abide by Rule 405 NYSE, presenters should abide by presentation Rule 1:

Understand your audience.

TIPS TO LEARN MORE ABOUT YOUR AUDIENCE

Do your homework. Take time to research and study your audience. By doing so, you will be better prepared to speak to the issues, concerns, goals and fears that are important to your audience.

- Talk with people within the organization.
- Ask lots of questions.
- Listen for information you can build into your presentation.
- Read their marketing material and brochures.
- Browse their Web site.
- Use an Internet search engine for information on individuals who will attend.
- Peruse annual reports for company values, mission statement, performance numbers . . .
- Scan periodicals for information pertaining to the company or its competitors.
- Watch for television reports.
- Visit their stores or offices.
- Get a copy of their most recent newsletter.
- Become familiar with terminology they dislike or avoid. Find out the terminology they prefer. "We don't use the term 'outsource'; we prefer to call it 'off shoring.'"
- Gather information on the business, the competition and the industry. Use what fits your theme or message.
- Peruse local business journals.

QUESTIONS TO ASK

- Who will be in attendance? How many? Get a list of names, titles, roles and responsibilities.

- Will the decision-maker be in the room? Will the decision maker be there for the entire presentation or part of the presentation? What might cause her to miss it or leave before it is over?

- What are their expectations? What needs to be done to meet their expectations?

- What is the meeting theme?

- What agenda items come before and after your remarks?

- What is the expected attire? Is it formal, business, business casual or casual. When asking about attire, be sure to find out as much as you can. Business casual can mean different things to different groups. Casual to some is wool slacks, jackets and ties.

- Do the attendees get along? Do they laugh easily?

- What do the attendees have in common?

- How is the information you are going to cover relevant to the attendees?

- How might the information help the attendees?

- What are the starting and ending times for the meeting?

- What is the seating arrangement and can it be changed?

- Is it a neutral, friendly or hostile audience?

- What do they know about your topic?

- What do they know about you, the presenter?

Researching and asking questions takes less time than you might think and your work will pay big dividends.

In two or three phone calls, you can ask all of these questions. In many cases, they will volunteer additional information. Be as conversational and curious as possible when asking the questions. Try not to make it sound like an interrogation. State up front that you need the information to ensure a productive meeting. Most organizations are happy to provide the information. They too want the meeting to be productive.

>> The quickest way to connect with an audience is by demonstrating that you understand their business, their issues and their concerns.

In addition to business opportunities, follow this crucial rule when interviewing for a job. Job fairs give graduate and under-graduate students a chance to talk face-to-face with prospective employers. The total lack of knowledge by many students about what the companies do is a consistent "pet peeve" of employers. The student will lead off with, "So, what do you guys do?"

You heighten your odds of connecting when you "Know Your Audience."

CHAPTER NINE
PRACTICE

"We are what we repeatedly do. Excellence, then, is not an act,
but a habit."
—Aristotle

IF I CANNOT PERSUADE YOU TO PRACTICE, I cannot help you to improve.

The skills discussed in this book are quite basic. Mastering these skills is a matter of making them habits. Once they become habit, they will not fail you, even under the most extreme pressure and the most adverse circumstances.

When placed in pressure situations, our bodies seek comfort. If you are most comfortable with your hands in your pockets, then that is where your hands will go when an audience member nails you with a tough question. If you are most comfortable looking down at the floor while thinking, that is where your eyes will go when a client asks you to justify your fees.

"No matter who you are, no matter how good an athlete you are, we're creatures of habit. The better your habits are, the better they'll be in pressure situations."
  —Hockey great Wayne Gretsky

"Every great shot you hit, you've already hit a bunch of times in practice."
  —Martina Navratilova, winner of 167 singles tennis titles, including a record nine at Wimbledon

Practice is a critical component of being successful in any field of endeavor. Consider the following:

During a regulation National Football League game, each team will run on average 65 offensive plays. The average play, from the snap of the ball until the official blows the whistle to end the play, lasts approximately 5 ½ seconds. Using these numbers, during a regulation game an NFL offensive or defensive player is actually playing football for about 6 minutes. This is the amount of time the ball is in play. This does not include the time they are in the huddle, timeouts, doing a celebratory dance, drinking Gatorade on the sideline, strategizing at halftime, TV timeouts, or waiting for an official to review a play. Only 6 minutes of playing time.

On a side note, based on their salaries, what does an NFL player make per minute? Are you thinking that maybe you're in the wrong profession?

My main point here is not about how much NFL players make or how little time they spend playing the game. NFL players practice 6 days a week. Their days consist of meetings to cover offensive and defensive strategy, strength and conditioning training, on-the-field practice time, film study and rehabilitation. Jim Lippencott, the Director of Football Operations for the Cincinnati Bengals, estimates that during the season an NFL quarterback will put in

50 to 60 hours per week, if not more, practicing and preparing for each game. All those hours of practice and preparation for 6 minutes of playing time. Is it worth it? What happens in those six minutes determines the winners from the losers and the champions from those who say, "Wait until next year."

Amanda Borden was Captain of the 1996 Olympics Gold Medal USA Gymnastics team. Her training for a single event, such as the balance beam, included over 5000 repetitions of the entire routine and over 100,000 repetitions of the various skills (hand movements, turns, dismount . . .).

Janet Evans, three-time Olympian and winner of four Olympic gold medals in swimming, swam twelve miles a day, six days a week during her twelve-year Olympic pursuit. That's approximately 45,000 miles of practice.

Byron Janise, renowned internationally as one of the world's greatest concert pianists of all time, once stated that if he missed one day of practice, he could tell. If he missed two days of practice, his coach could tell. If he missed three days of practice, his audience could tell.

The exciting thing about practicing these skills is that you don't need an audience. You don't need props. You don't need equipment. The only thing you need is the desire to improve.

Throughout this book I have listed practice opportunities that you can include in your normal daily routines. If you take advantage of the opportunities, you will improve quickly. If you don't take advantage of the opportunities, then these skills will NEVER become second nature. They will NEVER become part of your presentation arsenal.

The stronger your habits, the more consistent and effective you will be under the pressure of presenting and conducting question and answer sessions.

Repetition is critical but does not always guarantee improvement. As John Kilcullen, founder of the *For Dummies* brand books, said, "Just because you're doing something a lot, doesn't mean you're getting better. You might simply be reinforcing bad habits."

>> Those who practice improve. Those who don't, don't.

There are places where practicing eye contact is ill-advised.

EXERCISE:

Write down the approximate percentage of your working day that you spend communicating and presenting. This includes conversations, meetings, phone calls, voice mail and every other venue in which you are speaking or listening.

Communicating _____ %

Now, write down the approximate percentage of time you spend practicing to improve your communication skills.

Practicing _____ %

When participants in my workshops fill out their percentages, I typically see the following results:

Communicating—the average response is 50% to 80%.

Practicing—the average response is 0% to 2%.

Most people spend absolutely no time practicing. Yet they communicate 50–80% of the time.

Following and in the back of the book are weekly practice charts. Begin today to document where, what and how often you practice. The more you practice, the sooner you will become exceptional.

DELIVERY SKILLS WEEKLY PRACTICE CHART

Week of: _____

Note where you practiced.   If you practice the skill, check the box.

	Posture	Gestures	Eye Contact	Voice Volume	Inflection	Filler
Monday Comments:						
Tuesday Comments:						
Wednesday Comments:						
Thursday Comments:						
Friday Comments:						
Saturday Comments:						
Sunday Comments:						

Additional observations: _____

Who impressed you with their skills? _____

Why? _____

Who did not impress you? _____

Why? _____

CHAPTER TEN

QUICK ON YOUR FEET: CONDUCTING SUCCESSFUL Q&A SESSIONS

IF YOUR PRESENTATION IS TO BE A SUCCESS, then your question and answer session (Q&A) must be conducted professionally.

Q&A is an opportunity to build rapport, find out what is on the minds of your audience members, and share material you didn't have time to build into your presentation.

>> The credibility of a presenter can rise or fall during Q&A.

Q&A is perhaps the most significant segment of your presentation. During Q&A, you will find out if your message is getting through. Are they interested? Do they agree or disagree with your position? Are they engaged? A strong presentation can be overshadowed by a less than stellar Q&A session. In fact, it wasn't a strong presentation if the Q&A flopped.

In many situations your presentation will be a rolling Q&A session. People will ask questions throughout most presentations. Encouraging questions during the presentation can be effective, but it requires greater attention to time constraints. If your presentation is to last 10 minutes, it's a good idea to ask the audience to hold their questions until the end. A 3-minute question in the middle of a 10-minute presentation can make a significant dent in the amount of material you are able to cover. It can also break your momentum and divert the flow of information.

Think back to the CEO I mentioned in Chapter Six who improved his Q&A effectiveness by observing the verbal and non-verbal cues from his audience as they asked him questions? Observing these cues will give you a head start in understanding the intent behind the questions.

Let's approach Q&A from a position of strength and experience rather than surprise and retreat.

Q&A TIPS AND TECHNIQUES

Composure, Composure, Composure

Maintain your composure at all times. We tend to react adversely to the unknown or the unexpected. We can never be totally prepared for every question, but we can anticipate questions and practice our responses to those questions.

By maintaining your composure, you are able to think clearly and respond appropriately. If you lose your cool, you will most likely lose credibility with the audience.

It is critical during Q&A that your non-verbal skills are strong and second nature. Our natural response to pressure is to move away from the source of pressure.

Maintain a "move forward" attitude during Q&A sessions. Do not retreat. Maintain strong body language. This is especially true when the questions become more difficult or more aggressive.

Read Your Audience

Watch the body language, facial expressions, voice projection and inflection of the person asking the question. If you are observant, you can get a good feel for the intent of the question. Is she asking the question because she is confused? Does she need clarification? Is she challenging me with the question? Is she eager to hear more?

By watching body language and listening to tone of voice, you can quickly discern a friendly question from a hostile question. You can distinguish a question based on misunderstanding from a question based on curiosity.

Rehearse, Rehearse, Rehearse

Conduct mock Q&A sessions prior to your presentation. Ask members of your organization to play the role of the audience. Have them fire questions at you from all angles. Encourage them to hit you with the toughest possible questions. Encourage them to challenge your responses. Practice rapid-fire, unfair and uninformed questions. Convince one person to play the audience jerk. You'll probably have several volunteers for that role.

If you don't have a group available to help you conduct a mock Q&A, write down questions on 3 × 5 cards, shuffle the cards and answer the questions as they are dealt. Practice as if it were the real Q&A. If you will be standing during your presentation, then stand when you practice. Work the room as if it were the actual presentation. Practice moving toward your audience. Practice repeating and rephrasing questions. Work on your eye contact (even if the eye contact is with chairs when you practice). The more accurately you can simulate the Q&A, the more effective you will be when you go live.

Mock sessions are worth their weight in gold. Answers tend to be smoother when we've said them two or three times. How we think about an answer and how we actually verbalize that answer can be surprisingly different.

Politicians spend a considerable amount of time preparing for debates. They understand that a single response can make or break the debate and possibly make or break the election.

Rehearsing Q&A is an excellent way to avoid post-presentation regrets—those inner thoughts you want to scream out:

"Why didn't I think of that until I left the room?"

"Can you believe that I forgot to mention . . . ?"

"What was I thinking not to mention our work with the _____ account?"

Know Your Audience

The more you know about your audience, the better prepared you will be for Q&A.

Respect Your Audience

Respect all questions. Even when you're sure you're right and the audience member is wrong, don't go for the jugular. It's not worth the short-lived gratification. Your ego will be gratified, but your credibility will be grounded. Earn respect by respecting others and by handling an unprofessional attack with poise and professionalism.

Take Charge

Stand your ground with the calm and presence of a seasoned professional.

Q&A REMINDERS

The best thing you can do to ensure a successful Q&A is to effectively frame your presentation when you first begin speaking. By doing so, you start with a clear purpose, you can stay on point and you can redirect off-topic questions.

- Encourage participation.
- Understand the question, or don't answer the question. Ask for clarification, ask the person to define part of the question, request that the person give you an example to illustrate the question, or turn to the other members of the group to see if they could help you understand the question.
- Multiple part questions. Answer questions one part at a time. Don't burden yourself by trying to remember and then answer a three- or four-part question. Break down the question. "What was part one of your question?" Answer part one and move on to part two of the question, part three . . .

If you are asked a three-part question, choose the part you want to respond to first. This gives you additional time to think about your responses to the other parts of the question.

- Repeat or rephrase the question.

  "Let me make sure I understand your question." "If I understand your question, you're asking me . . ."

  "The question, for those who did not hear it was . . ."

  "To clarify, are you wanting to know more about . . .?"

- Involve everyone. Repeat and answer the question to the entire group. DO NOT answer the entire question with your eye contact solely fixed on the person who asked the question. Presenters who do this tend to lose the rest of the audience. It is quite natural to give more eye contact to the person who asked the question. Just don't make your eye contact exclusive to that person.

- At the end of an answer, ask the questioner, "Does that answer your question?" You may not want to use this technique if the person asking the questions has been a burr in your Q&A saddle. Simply move on to the next question.

- Stay in control! Keep the information relevant. Don't allow an audience member to change the direction of your presentation and Q&A. The more defined you are at the beginning of your presentation about the topic and your objectives, the easier it is to cut off questions that don't match those objectives.

- Keep it simple. Answer the question and move on. Don't dwell, don't ramble, don't try to tell them everything you know.

- Use names to personalize your answers. "Brenda's question has to do with . . ." "Jeff asked a question regarding . . ."

- Maintain strong body language. Move forward and maintain eye contact, even on the toughest, most aggressive questions. Don't retreat.

- Be aware of your eye contact. Lock-on to the questioner while she asks the question. Avoid glancing at the ceiling or the floor. Eyes speak volumes as to one's confidence level. Try to maintain eye contact as you respond.

- Don't fidget, dance, shuffle or get defensive. Keep your cool. They might simply be testing to see how you react.

- Neutralize a negative question. Question: "Why are your fees so ridiculously high?" Do not reinforce the negative by stating: "The question for those who didn't hear it was, 'Why are our fees so ridiculously high?'" Instead, use your restatement of the question to neutralize the negative: "Your question has to do with how we structure our fees, let me . . ."

- Correct inaccuracies, "I didn't say that."

- Correct false assumptions, "It would be a mistake for you to assume anything from what I just said other than what I just said."

- Correct inaccurate conclusions, "I think you're making a mistake to draw a conclusion."

- Based on the sensitivity of the information, consider what you will discuss, cannot discuss, and will not discuss.

- Be alert for questions you are not qualified to answer. It's a bad idea to answer legal questions if you are not an attorney or tax questions if you lack the credentials. Some people feel compelled to respond even if they are not qualified.

- If you don't know, don't bluff. Set it up early in your presentation that you might not have all the answers to all of their questions right now. You will, however, find the answers and get back with them. Give them a specific time frame in which you will get back with the answer. This builds credibility.

If you are caught bluffing, simply pack your bags and depart. You will have little, if any, credibility with the audience.

Dateline: San Jose, CA—A participant in a CEO boot camp told me that he ALWAYS comes up with an answer, whether he has one or not. I asked him if he has ever been caught bluffing. He said he had been caught bluffing one time.

He was delivering a funding presentation to a group of venture capitalists (VCs). Five minutes into the presentation one of the VCs interrupted saying, "Ed, did you know that Microsoft is developing this same technology? How can you begin to compete with Microsoft?" Our CEO was caught off guard. He had no idea that Microsoft was developing a similar product. But that didn't stop him from trying to bluff his way through a response. He launched into a comparison of his company's technology and Microsoft's technology. His product was better because of this, this and this. Microsoft's doesn't do this, this and this.

Three minutes into Ed's response the VC spoke up again. "You know what? I was thinking about a different technology. Microsoft isn't developing anything like your product."

Oops! Ed was caught in a bluff. For three minutes he compared his product to a phantom product. Everyone in the room knew he was bluffing. He had entered the room hoping to secure a $2,000,000 investment. He left the room with the exact amount of money he had in his wallet at the start of the meeting.

Bluffing destroys trust. Don't do it.

BUYING TIME TO GATHER YOUR THOUGHTS

Sometimes you need a few seconds to think about an answer before responding. You might need 15 to 30 seconds to formulate an appropriate response. It is better to stop and think than to begin your answer hemming and hawing until you finally find your direction. Your audience will know you're dancing, and your answer will have less impact.

Take your time. The human brain can sort through an incredible amount of information in three to five seconds if you maintain your composure and let your brain do its job. Resist the urge to fill the air with words that are yet to be formed into a cohesive thought.

- Pause. This is your most powerful tool. Use it. Pausing to think through your response is a sign that you are reflecting on the question. Be consistent. Pause whether the question is difficult or easy.

"Silence is golden when you can't think of a good answer."
—Muhammad Ali, *More Than a Hero*

Three seconds of silence to a nervous speaker feels like an eternity. Three seconds of silence to a confident speaker feels natural.

Former President Bill Clinton is a master of the pause. In both of the 1992 and 1996 presidential debates, he would pause with every question. It didn't matter if the question was difficult or easy. He would pause, move toward the person asking the question and then respond.

- **The extended pause** comes into play when you realize that it will take at least ten seconds to formulate your response. Let your audience know that you are going to think through your response. Take as much time as you need. "Let me think about that before I respond."

  A pause is a sign of confidence. Many people cannot handle silence when they are expected to be speaking or responding.

  Try this technique occasionally. When someone asks you a question, simply pause and look at the person as if you are waiting for more information. Maintain eye contact. The person asking the question will feel compelled to provide additional information. The silence, as you wait, is on their clock. The pressure is on them to fill the void. This technique allows you to gain additional insight as to the reason they are asking the question.

  A typical addition to the original question might be, "The reason I'm asking is because . . ." or "What I'm trying to get at is . . ." Now you've heard the question and the person has told you why they've asked it.

  Some questions are not well thought out, and this is a technique to flush out information that will help you generate the appropriate response.

- **Repeat or rephrase the question** as a courtesy to others in the room. "Let me make sure I understand your question . . ." "If I understand your question, you're asking me . . ." "Allow me to repeat your question." "For those who did not hear the question, it had to do with . . ."

- **Ask the questioner to repeat the question.** Limit the use of this technique. Save it for when you truly do not hear the question. If overused, it can appear an obvious stall tactic. It can also give the impression that the presenter is not intelligent enough to understand the question the first time through.

- **Return to the topic later.** "Let's come back to that later." "Kim, remind me to revisit that after the break." "If you could hold that question, we'll be covering that topic in the next segment."

- **Open the question to the group.** Use when appropriate (training, seminars, situations where you are trying to encourage participation). It would not be appropriate, for example, in a proposal situation as you present to the CEO, CFO and Senior VP. "OK, Bill asked the question, why are our fees so ridiculously high. Does anyone want to respond to that question?"

- **Ask them a question.** "What did you do in that situation?" "Amy, does your question pertain to our discussion yesterday?"

- **Find out why they are asking the question.** "And the reason you are asking that question?" "Specifically what would you like to know?" "And your question is?" "Why do you ask?" It is important when using this technique to use the appropriate tone of voice. Use a tone of voice that implies that you are doing your best to discern what they would like to know.

- **Ask them to define part of the question.** "Jill, define for me what you meant by the word variables."

- **Take a sip of water.** Try not to take your first sip of water immediately after hearing a difficult question.

- **Take a break** if the timing is right.

TEAM PRESENTATIONS AND Q&A

Determine who will answer questions on specific topics during your rehearsals. Don't stare at each other waiting for your teammate to answer a question.

If you're going to direct a question to a member of your team, first say the name of the team member to whom you are directing the question. This alerts the person just in case they've been napping. Repeat the question in order to give your teammate time to formulate her response.

Make your teammates look good. Do not correct them in a way that can remotely be interpreted as condescending. Partners have been known to destroy the credibility of managers by stepping in and correcting the manager in front of the client. Sometimes the correction is necessary in order to avoid misstating the situation. But tone of voice, body language and word choice make the difference between the manager feeling OK about the correction or feeling completely crushed.

Pay particular attention to the "Keep It Simple" rule when presenting as a team. Team members frequently feel compelled to elaborate on an answer that is already complete. In an effort to add compelling information, demonstrate their depth of knowledge, assert their authority, or show that they are paying attention, team members jump in and restate points that have already been made. Typically each person will put a personal twist on the restatement. This tends to cloud the issue or confuse the listener.

EXCEPTIONAL Q&A: BRITISH PRIME MINISTER TONY BLAIR

Few people communicate as effectively in Q&A sessions as Tony Blair. Tune into any interview or press conference featuring the British Prime Minister, and you will see what I mean.

Tony Blair exudes enthusiasm and professionalism. He radiates confidence and speaks in a conversational tone, even when reading a script. His message rings of optimism. He gestures freely and effectively. He smiles readily. Any and all questions are welcome. He stands tall and always stands his ground. His eye contact is direct, and he shares it with as much of the audience as possible. It is rare to hear Tony Blair utter an "um" or "uh." People with a clear and well-defined message typically do not use "verbal graffiti." He is as effective off the cuff as he is off a script. Prime Minister Blair has a good sense of humor and will use it to build rapport, disarm an adversary or keep an opponent off balance. Anyone who has watched Tony Blair during Prime Minister's Questions on C-SPAN understands the need to be "quick on your feet" and possess a quick wit during these House of Commons sessions. Prime Minister Blair is animated, dynamic and highly effective. People often ask me who they can watch to observe exceptional presentation skills in action. Watch Tony Blair.

CHAPTER ELEVEN
USING NERVOUS ENERGY TO CREATE POSITIVE RESULTS

"Public speaking is one of the best things I hate."

—Baseball great Yogi Berra

SWEATY PALMS, BEADS ON YOUR FOREHEAD AND UPPER LIP, racing pulse, tight stomach, dry mouth, shortness of breath, wobbly knees, shaking hands, sudden lapses of memory and the impulse to flee. Isn't public speaking fun?

It has long been said that public speaking is listed as the number one fear in the *Book of Lists*. Many people would rather be stung repeatedly by a swarm of killer bees than to stand up and deliver a speech.

Comedian Jerry Seinfeld suggests that the next time you attend a funeral, think about this: the person in the coffin is more relaxed than the person who has to deliver the eulogy.

Nervousness is a reaction to pressure and our desire to perform to the best of our ability. Ask any world-class performer in any field of endeavor, and the vast majority will admit that they get nervous prior to a performance. It's the competitive drive, the will to win and the fear of failure. Why do we get nervous prior to, and sometimes during, a presentation? Presenting to a group is not something most people do every day.

The possibility of sounding incompetent can make anyone apprehensive. If you are a professional, you want to perform to your highest level. There's always a chance that during your presentation, you will:

- Fall on your face—literally or figuratively.
- Make a major gaffe.
- Freeze up and forget your message.
- Face an audience member who knows more about your topic than you.
- Be stumped by questions from the audience.

YOU'RE NOT DIFFERENT—MOST PEOPLE GET NERVOUS

- Mikhail Baryshnikov, perhaps the world's most renowned dancer, admitted that he gets so nervous before performances, he feels physically ill. He doesn't know why. He can't stand the fact that it happens. But it happens.
- Lifelong actress Helen Hayes said that the day she didn't get nervous before a performance would be the day she would

retire. If she reached a point where she wasn't nervous, it meant that she did not care enough about the audience.

- Johnny Carson said he was nervous every night prior to his *Tonight Show* monologue. He did over 4000 shows.

THE MENTAL GAME OF PRESENTING

Many people claim that presenting makes them feel like they're standing in a spotlight, all eyes trained on their every move. Any mistake will be noted and archived in a permanent record.

Unless you are the sitting Federal Reserve Chairman, people are not hanging on your every word. Take comfort in knowing that most audiences are not paying that close of attention to your presentation.

>> If you make a minor mistake or miscue, your audience will probably not even notice.

FOCUS THE SPOTLIGHT ON YOUR MESSAGE AND YOUR AUDIENCE

Approach your presentation with the mindset that, "This message is important to this group. I will do everything in my power to help them understand and remember the message."

This mindset enables you to direct your energy to bringing out the message. It also enables you to assist the audience in understanding what you have to say.

It's not about you. It's about the message.

Mental Approach:

Option A—"Oh my gosh, every eye in the place is staring at me. I have to stand here for thirty minutes and speak to this group."

Option B—"I have critical information that can make a positive difference for the people in this room. I have thirty minutes to help them understand this information. Let's get started."

CONVERT NERVOUS ENERGY TO POSITIVE ENERGY

Pre-presentation nerves are what drive us to prepare more than we would if we were totally relaxed approaching a presentation. Nervousness keeps us alert and provides a boost of adrenaline.

Work to channel your nervous energy into crisp, well-defined gestures and movements. Convert your nervous energy to greater voice projection and inflection. Tap your nervous energy to encourage participation so you are not standing in the spotlight, but shining the spotlight on your message.

TECHNIQUES FOR CONTROLLING THE FEAR

Two-minute Drill

Memorize your first two minutes. I don't necessarily mean word for word. Practice your first two minutes repeatedly until they flow smoothly. The exact words may change slightly with each attempt, but your message is clear and consistent.

Feeling completely comfortable that your opening is solid and secure will be a tremendous help in calming the jitters.

Don't change the opening of your presentation at the last minute unless absolutely necessary.

Cheat Sheets

If you need to have notes nearby or with you, by all means do so. You don't have to rely completely on your memory. If you do carry notes, however, don't lock your eyes onto your notes and become dependent on them throughout your presentation.

Rehearse, Rehearse, Rehearse

There is no substitute for rehearsal. Rehearse out loud. Visualize your audience in front of you while you rehearse. If you will be using visual aids, use them as you rehearse.

How many times have you heard someone say, "I'm better 'off the cuff' than I am if my presentation is rehearsed." In all of the coaching I have done, I have yet to work with anyone who is better "off the cuff" than they are when they've had an opportunity to practice and go through the presentation out loud.

Rehearse in Three-minute Segments

Rehearsing your presentation from start to finish can get tiresome quickly. The start-to-finish method allows fewer opportunities to adjust and adapt your material. Break the presentation into three-minute segments. Work on each segment multiple times. Be sure to work on your transitions from one segment to the next.

This approach will allow you to refine the material. It will also enable you to adjust the content on the fly. You can easily remove segments that you find do not apply to your audience. You can skip ahead to a specific segment if a question pertaining to that segment is asked. The segmented approach also allows you to keep more accurate track of how your presentation times out.

It's OK to Forget

Lapses of memory happen to the very best performers. Don't let it throw you. Assume that you will have an occasional memory lapse or "brain cramp." Pause, glance down at your notes, gather your thoughts, look up and continue your presentation.

Don't Try to Tell Them Everything You Know

People tend to feel the need to pass along every detail of their topic to anyone willing to listen. Your audience doesn't want to know everything you know. Keep it simple. If they want more detail, they will ask for it.

Reduce your material—If your presentation is scheduled to last 20 minutes, don't try to deliver 25 minutes of material. Be prepared with 17 minutes of material and allow time for flexibility and spontaneity. No one will complain if you finish two minutes early.

Don't feel compelled to cover every item in detail during your presentation. That's why there's Q&A. Q&A allows you to touch on material you were unable to cover in the allotted time.

Arrive an Hour Early

Give yourself time to prepare and relax. Remember our 60-20 Rule. Arrive 60 minutes early so that you can relax. Meet and greet for the 20 minutes prior to your presentation.

Mingle

Meet as many participants as possible. Build some allies prior to your presentation.

Visualize Success

Picture yourself delivering an exceptional speech.

The Blue Angels, the precision flying team of the United States Navy, have briefing meetings prior to EVERY performance. They consider the briefings to be a very important part of performing successful and safe demonstrations.

Prior to every show, the Blue Angels team meets in a briefing room. The #1 pilot says everything that he is going to say in the air. All of the pilots close their eyes and visualize what it's going to look like. If they are doing a loop, the #1 pilot will go through every single voice call that he's going to make on the radios, and all of the pilots visualize what the loop is going to look like. By the end of the briefing, they have flown the entire demonstration, the entire show, before they even get into their jets.*

Neil Rock is a nationally known author and expert on goal setting and visualization. Neil has used goal setting and visualization to become an All-American collegiate track star, earn an MBA, achieve perennial top achiever status in sales and break performance records as a manager for one of the most successful companies in the world. In his book, *How to Catch a Road Runner*, Neil discusses how to achieve goals through visualization, writing down your goals and keeping them visible.

In Neil's words, "The mind doesn't know the difference between actual performance and what we visualize in vivid detail."

---

* from "The Blue Angels—In Pursuit of Excellence," Dreams Come True Productions
  www.dctproductions.com

Visualize yourself delivering the presentation. Visualize the room you will be presenting in. Visualize your audience. Picture yourself in front of the audience feeling confident, prepared and relaxed. Then do as the Blue Angels do, go through your entire presentation out loud.

I know an attorney who goes to the courtroom the evening before every court appearance. He practices his opening argument, his witness questioning and his closing argument exactly as he will deliver them during the trial. He knows where he will stand when addressing the jury, the judge and each witness. His success in the courtroom is frequent, and his courtroom presence is impressive.

Visualize yourself delivering an organized, passionate, engaging presentation in a conversational manner, and it will be so.

Breathe Deeply

Deep breathing helps relax your body.

Take a Walk—Get Some Exercise

Studies show that exercise can help to relax your system for two hours or more following the exercise. Take a brisk walk prior to departing for your presentation.

Be Yourself

We all have different presentation styles. Don't try to be someone else. Let your personality flow. I have witnessed presenters who feel compelled to be funny because the presenter before them was funny. Don't force it! As President George Bush, Sr. used to say, "Stay the course." Be yourself. Stick with your style and your material.

Be Careful What You Eat and Drink

Because nervousness ties stomachs in knots and makes mouths dry, avoid:

- **Eating a large meal just prior to presenting**: It's better to have your blood flowing to your brain during the presentation than having your body's energy directed to digesting that 22-ounce flank steak you just engulfed. Nervousness and a full stomach can add up to trouble.

- **Caffeine**: It affects different people in different ways. If you are nervous or edgy, the last thing you want is to multiply that edge with a dose of caffeine.

- **Carbonated drinks**: When it comes to carbonation, what goes down must come up.

- **Ice water or cold drinks**: Your throat should be kept warm and moist. Because cold drinks tighten the throat, the safest drink is room temperature water. Decaffeinated tea, coffee and hot chocolate are also good choices.

- **Dairy products**: In addition to potential intolerance, dairy drinks tend to disrupt the normal flow of fluids in our mouths. They tend to glob our fluids together and make it difficult to enunciate.

- **Fruit juices that are highly acidic**: If it sounds like the presenter has something caught in her throat, chances are good that she is drinking cranberry juice, lemonade, orange juice or another form of fruit drink.

CHAPTER TWELVE
YOUR INTRODUCTION IS IMPORTANT

AN EFFECTIVE INTRODUCTION SHOULD:

- Build the credibility of the speaker.
- Create anticipation for the speaker and her topic.
- Heighten the relevance of the topic to the audience.
- Be as brief as possible. Let the speaker speak.

Most introductions are ineffective. Most people don't introduce others often, and they don't spend the appropriate time preparing.

When you are the speaker being introduced:

Type your introduction in paragraph form, using a font size that is easy to read, 18 to 22. Send your introduction to the person who is scheduled to introduce you. Call that person to see if he needs any clarification and to have him read your introduction back to you. This prevents the awkward moment when he completely hacks up your name in front of the audience. A common sense and practical tip is to type the phonetic spelling of your name next to your name at the top of the introduction. My last name, Koegel, is frequently mispronounced. So on all of my introductions I write, Tim Koegel (pronounced Kay-Gull).

Say to the person introducing you, "At the very end of my introduction, would you, in your own words, highlight the importance and relevance of the presentation to the audience." This explanation seems to have more credibility coming from someone who is part of the group compared to coming from the speaker.

For example, the end of the introduction might sound something like this: "Everyone in this room understands that competition has become much more intense in the last 12 months. We know that in order to succeed, it is critical that we change the way we communicate our message. Today's speaker has a proven track record of improving the way organizations communicate. So let's give our full undivided attention to our speaker, Mr._____."

Or picture the person introducing you. He has just delivered your introduction. He takes off his reading glasses, looks up at the audience, pauses and says, "The timing of this presentation could not be better. Everyone in this room . . .

This small piece of ad-libbing builds your credibility and encourages the audience to give you their undivided attention.

These techniques personalize the introduction. The topic becomes more relevant to the audience.

The introduction should help the audience understand who you are and why it's important for them to listen carefully to your information.

When you are introducing someone:

Ask the speaker to write out his introduction. Then read it back to him. Do justice to the person you are introducing by practicing the introduction, out loud, at least five times. Highlight facts that the speaker deems relevant. Be as brief as possible. Use some of the same techniques listed above. Break from the script to remind your audience of the importance of the information and its relevance to what they do every day.

Never read the entire introduction with your head and eyes down. Your impact will be much greater if you deliver the introduction in a conversational manner. Look at your audience, and glance at your notes. Most people do the opposite. They glance occasionally at the audience and stare at their notes.

People introducing others tend to look repeatedly at the speaker as if to verify that the information being delivered is accurate. Avoid this. It will make you appear hesitant and uncertain about what you're doing.

If the speaker has provided a written introduction, do not start your remarks with, "Our speaker today has provided me with some information for her introduction." The reason for this is simple. Introductions highlight accomplishments, awards, honors received and the expertise of the speaker. By saying, "I'm going to read to you the introduction Katy just handed me," you are setting Katy up to look braggadocios. "Listen to all the great things Katy has to say about herself."

If you are unable to get a written introduction from the speaker, prepare the introduction yourself. Include The 3Ps of Introductions.

1. Professional background of the speaker—title, honors, awards, experience.

2. Personal background—family, hobbies, personal connection with you and the audience.

3. Purpose in speaking—relevance of the topic to the audience.

CHAPTER THIRTEEN

DO NOT ACCEPT AVERAGE WHEN YOU CAN BE EXCEPTIONAL

"Once you fly, you will walk with your eyes skyward. For there you have been and there you will go again."

—Leonardo da Vinci

THINK ABOUT THE SKILLS we have covered in this book. What specific skills would make the most immediate positive difference in your ability to communicate?

List in the order of priority the three skills you would like to improve most immediately.

I'm asking your commitment to focus on one skill for the next two weeks—every day, and every time you communicate.

I hope you are willing to make this commitment. If you commit to work on your top priority skill for the next 14 days, that skill will most likely become second nature. It will become a habit. Once it is a habit, it will not fail under pressure. It is your skill to use at will thereafter.

Then move on to the next skill on your priority list and make it second nature.

CONCLUSION

CONGRATULATIONS ON COMPLETING THE FIRST PART of your journey to becoming an exceptional presenter. What you do from this point will determine how quickly you reach the exceptional level. As you will soon come to see, improving your ability to present and persuade will affect every aspect of your life.

Please remember three things:

1. Do not accept average when you can be exceptional.

2. Every contact counts. Every interview counts. Every presentation counts.

3. Those who practice improve. Those who don't, don't.

Once you achieve exceptional, you will never again accept average.

Good luck.

PRESENTATION SHEETS

PERSONAL IMPROVEMENT GOALS

Today's Date _____

Overall Rating _____

How can I improve my overall rating? _____

	Date of Noticeable Improvement	Date of Significant Improvement	Date of Exceptional
Presence			
Posture			
Gestures 2nd Nature			
Eye Contact Shared and Sustained			
Movement— Visuals			
Voice Projection			
Inflection			
Filler Free			
Overall Effectiveness			

Game plan for achieving my improvement goals

_____

_____

PRESENTATION ASSESSMENT FORM

Rating scale 1 = not at all; 10 = exceptional

Presentation:

Was I **organized**? (1–10) _____

Strengths and deficiencies of my content? _____

_____

_____

Was my delivery **passionate**? (1–10) _____

Primary posture: (circle one or more):

Gestures and movement: Defined, nebulous or limited

Eye contact: Sustained for three to four seconds?   Y   N

               Shared—Did I involve everyone?   Y   N

Facial expressions: Inviting or reserved

Voice: Dynamic or monotone

Verbal graffiti/filler used: _____

Was I **engaging**? (1–10) _____

Engagement techniques used: _____

Was I **natural** and conversational? (1–10) _____

Overall rating (1–10) _____

Additional comments and observations: _____

_____

_____

PRESENTATION ASSESSMENT FORM

Rating scale 1 = not at all; 10 = exceptional

Presentation:

Was I **organized**? (1–10) _____

Strengths and deficiencies of my content? _____

_____

_____

Was my delivery **passionate**? (1–10) _____

Primary posture: (circle one or more):

Gestures and movement: Defined, nebulous or limited

Eye contact: Sustained for three to four seconds?   Y   N

Shared—Did I involve everyone?   Y   N

Facial expressions: Inviting or reserved

Voice: Dynamic or monotone

Verbal graffiti/filler used: _____

Was I **engaging**? (1–10) _____

Engagement techniques used: _____

Was I **natural** and conversational? (1–10) _____

Overall rating (1–10) _____

Additional comments and observations: _____

_____

_____

PRESENTATION ASSESSMENT FORM

Rating scale 1 = not at all; 10 = exceptional

Presentation:

Was I **organized**? (1 10) _____

Strengths and deficiencies of my content? _____

_____

_____

Was my delivery **passionate**? (1–10) _____

Primary posture: (circle one or more):

Gestures and movement: Defined, nebulous or limited

Eye contact: Sustained for three to four seconds?   Y   N

　　　　　　Shared—Did I involve everyone?   Y   N

Facial expressions: Inviting or reserved

Voice: Dynamic or monotone

Verbal graffiti/filler used: _____

Was I **engaging**? (1–10) _____

Engagement techniques used: _____

Was I **natural** and conversational? (1–10) _____

Overall rating (1–10) _____

Additional comments and observations: _____

_____

_____

DELIVERY SKILLS WEEKLY PRACTICE CHART

Week of: _____

Note where you practiced.   If you practice the skill, check the box.

	Posture	Gestures	Eye Contact	Voice Volume	Inflection	Filler
Monday Comments:						
Tuesday Comments:						
Wednesday Comments:						
Thursday Comments:						
Friday Comments:						
Saturday Comments:						
Sunday Comments:						

Additional observations: _____

Who impressed you with their skills? _____

Why? _____

Who did not impress you? _____

Why? _____

DELIVERY SKILLS WEEKLY PRACTICE CHART

Week of: _____

Note where you practiced.

If you practice the skill, check the box.

	Posture	Gestures	Eye Contact	Voice Volume	Inflection	Filler
Monday Comments:						
Tuesday Comments:						
Wednesday Comments:						
Thursday Comments:						
Friday Comments:						
Saturday Comments:						
Sunday Comments:						

Additional observations: _____

Who impressed you with their skills? _____

Why? _____

Who did not impress you? _____

Why? _____

DELIVERY SKILLS WEEKLY PRACTICE CHART

Week of: _____

Note where you practiced.   If you practice the skill, check the box.

	Posture	Gestures	Eye Contact	Voice Volume	Inflection	Filler
Monday Comments:						
Tuesday Comments:						
Wednesday Comments:						
Thursday Comments:						
Friday Comments:						
Saturday Comments:						
Sunday Comments:						

Additional observations: _____

Who impressed you with their skills? _____

Why? _____

Who did not impress you? _____

Why? _____

DELIVERY SKILLS WEEKLY PRACTICE CHART

Week of: _____

Note where you practiced.

If you practice the skill, check the box.

	Posture	Gestures	Eye Contact	Voice Volume	Inflection	Filler
Monday Comments:						
Tuesday Comments:						
Wednesday Comments:						
Thursday Comments:						
Friday Comments:						
Saturday Comments:						
Sunday Comments:						

Additional observations: _____

Who impressed you with their skills? _____

Why? _____

Who did not impress you? _____

Why? _____

DELIVERY SKILLS WEEKLY PRACTICE CHART

Week of: _____

Note where you practiced.   If you practice the skill, check the box.

	Posture	Gestures	Eye Contact	Voice Volume	Inflection	Filler
Monday Comments:						
Tuesday Comments:						
Wednesday Comments:						
Thursday Comments:						
Friday Comments:						
Saturday Comments:						
Sunday Comments:						

Additional observations: _____

Who impressed you with their skills? _____

Why? _____

Who did not impress you? _____

Why? _____

DELIVERY SKILLS WEEKLY PRACTICE CHART

Week of: _____

Note where you practiced.

If you practice the skill, check the box.

	Posture	Gestures	Eye Contact	Voice Volume	Inflection	Filler
Monday Comments:						
Tuesday Comments:						
Wednesday Comments:						
Thursday Comments:						
Friday Comments:						
Saturday Comments:						
Sunday Comments:						

Additional observations: _____

Who impressed you with their skills? _____

Why? _____

Who did not impress you? _____

Why? _____

OBSERVATION SHEET

We learn a great deal from observing others. Analyze guests being interviewed on TV shows such as *Meet the Press*, *This Week*, *Hardball*, *20/20*, *O'Reilly Factor*, *Crossfire*, and *60 Minutes*.

Show: _____   Date: _____

Guest: _____   Host: _____

Initial impression of guest: _____

Message was: Well defined/diluted/sidetracked

Why: _____

_____

Write the first two words or sounds of the guest's answers:

_____   _____   _____

Physical Presence

Fidgety? If so, how? _____

Were movements and gestures: Defined/limited/nebulous

Adjustments in chair: Frequent/noticeable/infrequent

Posture: Strong/passive/weak. Describe: _____

_____

_____

Eye contact: Sustained/fleeting

Voice: Unwavering/cautious/hesitant

Filler used and frequency: _____

Did content dictate comfort level? _____

If so, how? _____

Rate the effectiveness of the guest
(1 being disastrous and 10 being successful): _____

Overall observations: _____

_____

_____

OBSERVATION SHEET

We learn a great deal from observing others. Analyze guests being interviewed on TV shows such as *Meet the Press*, *This Week*, *Hardball*, *20/20*, *O'Reilly Factor*, *Crossfire*, and *60 Minutes*.

Show: _____   Date: _____

Guest: _____   Host: _____

Initial impression of guest: _____

Message was: Well defined/diluted/sidetracked

Why: _____

_____

Write the first two words or sounds of the guest's answers:

_____   _____   _____

Physical Presence

Fidgety? If so, how? _____

Were movements and gestures: Defined/limited/nebulous

Adjustments in chair: Frequent/noticeable/infrequent

Posture: Strong/passive/weak. Describe: _____

_____

_____

Eye contact: Sustained/fleeting

Voice: Unwavering/cautious/hesitant

Filler used and frequency: _____

Did content dictate comfort level? _____

If so, how? _____

Rate the effectiveness of the guest
(1 being disastrous and 10 being successful): _____

Overall observations: _____

_____

_____

PRESENTATION PREP SHEET

Presentation to: _____

Date: _____   Time: _____

What is the most important thing for your audience to remember?

_____

_____

_____

Structuring Your Presentation

My objective (Mission, Purpose, Goal) is:

_____

_____

_____

We are positioned as follows or the situation is as follows:

_____

_____

_____

**Ask if your understanding of the situation is correct.

The end result (Benefits, Consequences):

_____

_____

_____

Next step:

_____

_____

_____

Close with your Purpose Statement—"As you leave, I would like you to remember . . .

_____

_____

_____

_____

OUTLINE

Opening–Objective: _____

_____

_____

Body of Presentation

Point #1:

Support:

Point #2:

Support:

Point #3:

Support:

Summary: _____

_____

_____

Purpose Statement: _____

_____

_____

Helpful Info to Review

Who will lead the presentation? _____

What are the roles of team members? _____

Who will attend? _____

A/V requirements: _____

Handouts: _____

Stories/Anecdotes: _____

Contact name and number: _____

PRESENTATION PREP SHEET

Presentation to: _____

Date: _____   Time: _____

What is the most important thing for your audience to remember?

_____

_____

_____

Structuring Your Presentation

My objective (Mission, Purpose, Goal) is:

_____

_____

_____

We are positioned as follows or the situation is as follows:

_____

_____

_____

**Ask if your understanding of the situation is correct.

The end result (Benefits, Consequences):

_____

_____

_____

Next step:

_____

_____

_____

Close with your Purpose Statement—"As you leave, I would like you to remember . . .

_____

_____

_____

_____

OUTLINE

Opening–Objective: _____

_____

_____

Body of Presentation

Point #1:

Support:

Point #2:

Support:

Point #3:

Support:

Summary: _____

_____

_____

Purpose Statement: _____

_____

_____

Helpful Info to Review

Who will lead the presentation? _____

What are the roles of team members? _____

Who will attend? _____

A/V requirements: _____

Handouts: _____

Stories/Anecdotes: _____

Contact name and number: _____

PRESENTATION PREP SHEET

Presentation to: _____

Date: _____   Time: _____

What is the most important thing for your audience to remember?

_____

_____

_____

Structuring Your Presentation

My objective (Mission, Purpose, Goal) is:

_____

_____

_____

We are positioned as follows or the situation is as follows:

_____

_____

_____

**Ask if your understanding of the situation is correct.

The end result (Benefits, Consequences):

_____

_____

_____

Next step:

_____

_____

_____

Close with your Purpose Statement—"As you leave, I would like you to remember . . .

_____

_____

_____

_____

OUTLINE

Opening–Objective: _____

_____

_____

Body of Presentation

Point #1:

Support:

Point #2:

Support:

Point #3:

Support:

Summary: _____

_____

_____

Purpose Statement: _____

_____

_____

Helpful Info to Review

Who will lead the presentation? _____

What are the roles of team members? _____

Who will attend? _____

A/V requirements: _____

Handouts: _____

Stories/Anecdotes: _____

Contact name and number: _____

ABOUT THE AUTHOR

TIMOTHY KOEGEL has been a presentation and media consultant for two decades. His client list includes Fortune 500 companies, associations, business schools, political groups, early stage technology companies as well as leaders in sales and management.

His company, The Koegel Group, provides one-on-one coaching, group workshops and keynote presentations designed to improve the communication effectiveness and the message of those who attend.

Tim conducts boot camps nationally. He works with companies on venture funding presentations and IPO Road shows.

He is the founder of The Presentation Academy. He is also the owner of the Koegel Group Impact Speakers, a speaker's bureau booking appearances for celebrities, business leaders, sports figures, political personalities, coaches and trainers.

The Koegel Group is based in Washington, D.C.

Visit www.theexceptionalpresenter.com.

You will find updated techniques and information pertaining to the art of presenting. Share your thoughts on this book, your presentation experiences and your success stories.

Preview DVD training tools.

Listen to excerpts from *The Exceptional Presenter*™ audio series.

Learn how to bring *The Exceptional Presenter*™ training to your group or organization.

Order additional copies of *The Exceptional Presenter.*